Springfield College Reader

SECOND EDITION

Edited by Anne C. Wheeler

SPRINGFIELD COLLEGE

Cover image © Springfield College

www.kendallhunt.com
Send all inquiries to:
4050 Westmark Drive
Dubuque, IA 52004-1840

ISBN 978-1-5249-9381-8

Published in the United States of America

CONTENTS

INTRODUCTION

Dear Student,

Welcome to College Writing at Springfield College! The College Writing program plays an essential role in preparing students for reading, writing, and thinking in college and beyond. Over the course of the year, you will practice reading and writing in a variety of contexts. You will also engage in the writing process, and, through multiple drafts and revisions, you will develop your rhetorical and mechanical abilities. The goal of the College Writing program is not for you to "master writing," but rather to develop a strong understanding of how the process works and to become a flexible writer who is equipped to respond appropriately to a variety of writing situations.

In order to support your journey, this reader consists of a variety of readings that will either serve as models for the kind of writing that you may be asked to do or will provide direct instruction on various aspects of reading and writing. We've also included a number of essays written by Springfield College students during the time that they were enrolled in College Writing.

As you make your way through this reader, you will notice that many of the writer's employ, or recommend employing, the similar techniques. For example, notice how Claudia Rankin, author of "The Meaning of Serena Williams," which is in the **Writing With Research** section of the book intersperses her personal experience to launch analysis, as recommended in the **Narrative Writing** section. And while we have placed several essays with explicit advice about writing in the **Writerly Orientation** section, many of the essays offer explicit advice on how to—and how not to—write. As I said above, many of the essays in this book were written by students for their College Writing courses. They all model the kind of thoughtful, process-based writing that this reader, and our program, values.

I encourage you to take advantage of the strategies and techniques that your professors and peers offer you. I am so excited to see the work that you do!

Sincerely,

Anne C. Wheeler

Anne C. Wheeler, PhD
Assistant Professor of Composition & Rhetoric
Writing Program Director

PART 1

Narrative Writing

Critical Thinking in College: Writing From the Personal to the Academic

Gita DasBender

There is something about the term "critical thinking" that makes you draw a blank every time you think about what it means.* It seems so fuzzy and abstract that you end up feeling uncomfortable, as though the term is thrust upon you, demanding an intellectual effort that you may not yet have. But you know it requires you to enter a realm of smart, complex ideas that others have written about and that you have to navigate, understand, and interact with just as intelligently. It's a lot to ask for. It makes you feel like a stranger in a strange land.

As a writing teacher I am accustomed to reading and responding to difficult texts. In fact, I like grappling with texts that have interesting ideas no matter how complicated they are because I understand their value. I have learned through my years of education that what ultimately engages me, keeps me enthralled, is not just grammatically pristine, fluent writing, but writing that forces me to think beyond the page. It is writing where the writer has challenged herself and then offered up that challenge to the reader, like a baton in a relay race. The idea is to run with the baton.

You will often come across critical thinking and analysis as requirements for assignments in writing and upper-level courses in a variety of disciplines. Instructors have varying explanations of what they actually require of you, but, in general, they expect you to respond thoughtfully to texts you have read. The first thing you should remember is not to be afraid of critical thinking. It does *not* mean that you have to criticize the text, disagree with its premise, or attack the writer simply because you feel you must. Criticism is the process of responding to and evaluating ideas, argument, and style so that readers understand how and why you value these items.

Critical thinking is also a process that is fundamental to all disciplines. While in this essay I refer mainly to critical thinking in composition, the general principles behind critical thinking are strikingly similar in other fields and disciplines. In history, for instance, it could mean examining and analyzing primary sources in order to understand the context in which they were written. In the hard sciences, it usually involves careful reasoning, making judgments and decisions, and problem solving. While critical thinking may be subject-specific, that is to say, it can vary in method and technique depending on the discipline, most of its general principles such as rational thinking, making independent evaluations and judgments, and a healthy skepticism of what is being read, are common to all disciplines. No matter the area of study, the application of critical thinking skills leads to clear and flexible thinking and a better understanding of the subject at hand.

To be a critical thinker you not only have to have an informed opinion about the text but also a thoughtful response to it. There is no doubt that critical thinking is serious thinking, so here are some steps you can take to become a serious thinker and writer.

ATTENTIVE READING: A FOUNDATION FOR CRITICAL THINKING

A critical thinker is always a good reader because to engage critically with a text you have to read attentively and with an open mind, absorbing new ideas and forming your own as you go along. Let us imagine you are reading an essay by Annie Dillard, a famous essayist, called "Living like Weasels." Students are drawn to it because the idea of the essay appeals to something personally fundamental to all of us: how to live our lives. It is also a provocative essay that pulls the reader into the argument and forces a reaction, a good criterion for critical thinking. So let's say that in reading the essay you encounter a quote that gives you pause. In describing her encounter with a weasel in Hollins Pond, Dillard says, "I would like to learn, or remember, how to live . . . I don't think I can learn from a wild animal how to live in particular . . . but I might learn something of mindlessness, something of the purity of living in the physical senses and the dignity of living without bias or motive" (220). You may not be familiar with language like this. It seems complicated, and you have to stop ever so often (perhaps after every phrase) to see if you understood what Dillard means. You may ask yourself these questions:

- What does "mindlessness" mean in this context?
- How can one "learn something of mindlessness"?
- What does Dillard mean by "purity of living in the physical senses"?
- How can one live "without bias or motive"?

These questions show that you are an attentive reader. Instead of simply glossing over this important passage, you have actually stopped to think about what the writer means and what she expects you to get from it. Here is how I read the quote and try to answer the questions above: Dillard proposes a simple and uncomplicated way of life as she looks to the animal world for inspiration. It is ironic that she admires the quality of "mindlessness" since it is our consciousness, our very capacity to think and reason, which makes us human, which makes us beings of a higher order. Yet, Dillard seems to imply that we need to live instinctually, to be guided by our senses rather than our intellect. Such a "thoughtless" approach to daily living, according to Dillard, would mean that our actions would not be tainted by our biases or motives, our prejudices. We would go back to a primal way of living, like the weasel she observes. It may take you some time to arrive at this understanding on your own, but it is important to stop, reflect, and ask questions of the text whenever you feel stumped by it. Often such questions will be helpful during class discussions and peer review sessions.

LISTING IMPORTANT IDEAS

When reading any essay, keep track of all the important points the writer makes by jotting down a list of ideas or quotations in a notebook. This list not only allows you to remember ideas that are central to the writer's argument, ideas that struck you in some way or the other, but it also helps you to get a good sense of the whole reading assignment point by point. In reading Annie Dillard's essay, we come across several points that contribute toward her proposal for better living and that help us get a better understanding of her mainargument. Here is a list of some of her ideas that struck me as important:

1. "The weasel lives in necessity and we live in choice, hating necessity and dying at the last ignobly in its talons" (220).
2. "And I suspect that for me the way is like the weasel's: open to time and death painlessly, noticing everything, remembering nothing, choosing the given with a fierce and pointed will" (221).
3. "We can live any way we want. People take vows of poverty, chastity, and obedience—even of silence—by choice. The thing is to stalk your calling in a certain skilled and supple way, to locate the most tender and live spot and plug into that pulse" (221).
4. "A weasel doesn't 'attack' anything; a weasel lives as he's meant to, yielding at every moment to the perfect freedom of single necessity" (221).
5. "I think it would be well, and proper, and obedient, and pure, to grasp your one necessity and not let it go, to dangle from it limp wherever it takes you" (221).

These quotations give you a cumulative sense of what Dillard is trying to get at in her essay, that is, they lay out the elements with which she builds her argument. She first explains how the weasel lives, what she learns from observing the weasel, and then prescribes a lifestyle she admires—the central concern of her essay.

NOTICING KEY TERMS AND SUMMARIZING IMPORTANT QUOTES

Within the list of quotations above are key terms and phrases that are critical to your understanding of the ideal life as Dillard describes it. For instance, "mindlessness," "instinct," "perfect freedom of a single necessity," "stalk your calling," "choice," and "fierce and pointed will" are weighty terms and phrases, heavy with meaning, that you need to spend time understanding. You also need to understand the relationship between them and the quotations in which they appear. This is how you might work on each quotation to get a sense of its meaning and then come up with a statement that takes the key terms into account and expresses a general understanding of the text:

Quote 1: Animals (like the weasel) live in "necessity," which means that their only goal in life is to survive. They don't think about how they should live or what choices they should make like humans do. According to Dillard, we like to have options and resist the idea of "necessity." We fight death—an inevitable force that we have no control over—and yet ultimately surrender to it as it is the necessary end of our lives.

Quote 2: Dillard thinks the weasel's way of life is the best way to live. It implies a pure and simple approach to life where we do not worry about the passage of time or the approach of death. Like the weasel, we should live life in the moment, intensely experiencing everything but not dwelling on the past. We should accept our condition, what we are "given," with a "fierce and pointed will." Perhaps this means that we should pursue our one goal, our one passion in life, with the same single-minded determination and tenacity that we see in the weasel.

Quote 3: As humans, we can choose any lifestyle we want. The trick, however, is to go after our one goal, one passion like a stalker would after a prey.

Quote 4: While we may think that the weasel (or any animal) chooses to attack other animals, it is really only surrendering to the one thing it knows: its need to live. Dillard tells us there is "the perfect freedom" in this desire to survive because to her, the lack of options (the animal has no other option than to fight to survive) is the most liberating of all.

Quote 5: Dillard urges us to latch on to our deepest passion in life (the "one necessity") with the tenacity of a weasel and not let go. Perhaps she's telling us how important it is to have an unwavering focus or goal in life.

WRITING A PERSONAL RESPONSE: LOOKING INWARD

Dillard's ideas will have certainly provoked a response in your mind, so if you have some clear thoughts about how you feel about the essay this is the time to write them down. As you look at the quotes you have selected and your explanation of their meaning, begin to create your personal response to the essay. You may begin by using some of these strategies:

1. Tell a story. Has Dillard's essay reminded you of an experience you have had? Write a story in which you illustrate a point that Dillard makes or hint at an idea that is connected to her essay.
2. Focus on an idea from Dillard's essay that is personally important to you. Write down your thoughts about this idea in a first person narrative and explain your perspective on the issue.
3. If you are uncomfortable writing a personal narrative or using "I" (you should not be), reflect on some of her ideas that seem important and meaningful in general. Why were you struck by these ideas?
4. Write a short letter to Dillard in which you speak to her about the essay. You may compliment her on some of her ideas by explaining why you like them, ask her a question related to her essay and explain why that question came to you, and genuinely start up a conversation with her.

This stage in critical thinking is important for establishing your relationship with a text. What do I mean by this "relationship," you may ask? Simply put, it has to do with how you feel about the text. Are you amazed by how true the ideas seem to be, how wise Dillard sounds? Or are you annoyed by Dillard's let-me-tell-you-how-to-live approach and disturbed by the impractical ideas she so easily prescribes? Do you find Dillard's voice and style thrilling and engaging or merely confusing? No matter which of the personal response options you select, your initial reaction to the text will help shape your views about it.

MAKING AN ACADEMIC CONNECTION: LOOKING OUTWARD

First year writing courses are designed to teach a range of writing—from the personal to the academic—so that you can learn to express advanced ideas, arguments, concepts, or theories in any discipline. While the example I have been discussing pertains mainly to college writing, the method of analysis and approach to critical thinking I have demonstrated here will serve you well in a variety of disciplines. Since critical thinking and analysis are key elements of the reading and writing you will do in college, it is important to understand how they form a part of academic writing. No matter how intimidating the term "academic writing" may seem (it is, after all, associated with advanced writing and becoming an expert in a field of study), embrace it not as a temporary college requirement but as a habit of mind.

To some, academic writing often implies *impersonal* writing, writing that is detached, distant, and lacking in personal meaning or relevance. However, this is often not true of the academic writing you will do in a composition class. Here your presence as a writer—your thoughts, experiences, ideas, and therefore who you are—is of much significance to the writing you produce. In fact, it would not be far-fetched to say that in a writing class academic writing often begins with personal writing. Let me explain. If critical thinking begins with a personal view of the text, academic writing helps you broaden that view by going beyond the personal to a more universal point of view. In other words, academic writing often has its roots in one's private opinion or perspective about another writer's ideas but ultimately goes beyond this opinion to the expression of larger, more abstract ideas.

Your personal vision—your core beliefs and general approach to life—will help you arrive at these "larger ideas" or universal propositions that any reader can understand and be enlightened by, if not agree with. In short, academic writing is largely about taking a critical, analytical stance toward a subject in order to arrive at some compelling conclusions.

Let us now think about how you might apply your critical thinking skills to move from a personal reaction to a more formal academic response to Annie Dillard's essay. The second stage of critical thinking involves textual analysis and requires you to do the following:

- Summarize the writer's ideas the best you can in a brief paragraph. This provides the basis for extended analysis since it contains the central ideas of the piece, the building blocks, so to speak.
- Evaluate the most important ideas of the essay by considering their merits or flaws, their worthiness or lack of worthiness. Do not merely agree or disagree with the ideas but explore and explain why you believe they are socially, politically, philosophically, or historically important and relevant, or why you need to question, challenge, or reject them.
- Identify gaps or discrepancies in the writer's argument. Does she contradict herself? If so, explain how this contradiction forces you to think more deeply about her ideas. Or if you are confused, explain what is confusing and why.
- Examine the strategies the writer uses to express her ideas. Look particularly at her style, voice, use of figurative language, and the way she structures her essay and organizes her ideas. Do these strategies strengthen or weaken her argument? How?
- Include a second text—an essay, a poem, lyrics of a song—whose ideas enhance your reading and analysis of the primary text. This text may help provide evidence by supporting a point you're making, and further your argument.
- Extend the writer's ideas, develop your own perspective, and propose new ways of thinking about the subject at hand.

CRAFTING THE ESSAY

Once you have taken notes and developed a thorough understanding of the text, you are on your way to writing a good essay. If you were asked to write an exploratory essay, a personal response to Dillard's essay would probably suffice. However, an academic writing assignment requires you to be more critical. As counter-intuitive as it may sound, beginning your essay with a personal anecdote often helps to establish your relationship to the text and draw the reader into your writing. It also helps to ease you into the more complex task of textual analysis. Once you begin to analyze Dillard's ideas, go back to the list of important ideas and quotations you created as you read the essay. After a brief summary, engage with the quotations that are most important, that get to the heart of Dillard's ideas, and explore their meaning. Textual engagement, a seemingly slippery concept, simply means that you respond directly to some of Dillard's ideas, examine the value of Dillard's assertions, and explain why they are worthwhile or why they should be rejected. This should help you to transition into analysis and evaluation. Also, this part of your essay will most clearly reflect your critical thinking abilities as you are expected not only to represent Dillard's ideas but also to weigh their significance. Your observations about the various points she makes, analysis of conflicting viewpoints or contradictions, and your understanding of her general thesis should now be synthesized into a rich new idea about how we should live our lives. Conclude by explaining this fresh point of view in clear, compelling language and by rearticulating your main argument.

MODELING GOOD WRITING

When I teach a writing class, I often show students samples of really good writing that I've collected over the years. I do this for two reasons: first, to show students how another freshman writer understood and responded to an assignment that they are currently working on; and second, to encourage them to succeed as well. I explain that although they may be intimidated by strong, sophisticated writing and feel pressured to perform similarly, it is always helpful to see what it takes to get an A. It also helps to follow a writer's imagination, to learn how the mind works when confronted with a task involving critical thinking. The following sample is a response to the Annie Dillard essay. Figure 1 includes the entire student essay and my comments are inserted into the text to guide your reading.

Though this student has not included a personal narrative in his essay, his own worldview is clear throughout. His personal point of view, while not expressed in first person statements, is evident from the very beginning. So we could say that a personal response to the text need not always be expressed in experiential or narrative form but may be present as reflection, as it is here. The point is that the writer has traveled through the rough terrain of critical thinking by starting out with his own ruminations on the subject, then by critically analyzing and responding to Dillard's text, and finally by developing a strong point of view of his own about our responsibility as human beings. As readers we are engaged by clear, compelling writing and riveted by critical thinking that produces a movement of ideas that give the essay depth and meaning. The challenge Dillard set forth in her essay has been met and the baton passed along to us.

Work Cited

Dillard, Annie. "Living like Weasels." *One Hundred Great Essays*. Ed. Robert DiYanni. New York: Longman, 2002. 217–221. Print.

Building Our Lives: The Blueprint Lies Within

We all may ask ourselves many questions, some serious, some less important, in our lifetime. But at some point along the way, we all will take a step back and look at the way we are living our lives, and wonder if we are living them correctly. Unfortunately, there is no solid blueprint for the way to live our lives. Each person is different, feeling different emotions and reacting to different stimuli than the person next to them. Many people search for the true answer on how to live our lives, as if there are secret instructions out there waiting to be found. But the truth is we as a species are given a gift not many other creatures can claim to have: the ability to choose to live as we want, not as we were necessarily designed to. Even so, people look outside of themselves for the answers on how to live, which begs me to ask the question: what is wrong with just living as we are now, built from scratch through our choices and memories?

Comment: Even as the writer starts with a general introduction, he makes a claim here that is related to Dillard's essay.

Comment: The student asks what seems like a rhetorical question but it is one he will answer in the rest of his essay. It is also a question that forces the reader to think about a key term from the text—"choices."

Annie Dillard's essay entitled "Living Like Weasels" is an exploration into the way human beings might live, clearly stating that "We could live any way we want" (Dillard 211). Dillard's encounter with an ordinary weasel helped her receive insight into the difference between the way human beings live their lives and the way wild animals go about theirs. As a nature writer, Dillard shows us that we can learn a lot about the true way to live by observing nature's other creations. While we think and debate and calculate each and every move, these creatures just simply act. The thing that keeps human beings from living the purest life possible, like an animal such as the weasel, is the same thing that separates us from all wild animals: our minds. Human beings are creatures of caution, creatures of undeniable fear, never fully living our lives because we are too caught up with avoiding risks. A weasel, on the other hand, is a creature of action and instinct, a creature which lives its life the way it was created to, not questioning his motives, simply striking when the time to strike is right. As Dillard states, "the weasel lives in necessity and we live in choice, hating necessity and dying at the last ignobly in its talons" (Dillard 210).

Comment: Student summarizes Dillard's essay by explaining the ideas of the essay in fresh words.

Comment: Up until this point the student has introduced Dillard's essay and summarized some of its ideas. In the section that follows, he continues to think critically about Dillard's ideas and argument.

It is important to note and appreciate the uniqueness of the ideas Dillard presents in this essay because in some ways they are very true. For instance, it is true that humans live lives of caution, with a certain fear that has been built up continually through the years. We are forced to agree with Dillard's idea that we as humans "might learn something of mindlessness, something of the purity of living in the physical senses and the dignity of living without bias or motive" (Dillard 210). To live freely we need to live our lives with less hesitation, instead of intentionally choosing to not live to the fullest in fear of the consequences of our actions. However, Dillard suggests that we should forsake

Comment: This is a strong statement that captures the student's appreciation of Dillard's suggestion to live freely but also the ability to recognize why most people cannot live this way. This is a good example of critical thinking.

our ability of thought and choice all together. The human mind is the tool that has allowed a creature with no natural weapons to become the unquestioned dominant species on this plant ~~planet~~, and though it curbs the spontaneity of our lives, it is not something to be simply thrown away for a chance to live completely "free of bias or motive" (Dillard 210). We are a moral, conscious species, complete with emotions and a firm conscience, and it is the power of our minds that allows us to exist as we do now: with the ability to both think and feel at the same time. It grants us the ability to choose and have choice, to be guided not only by feelings and emotions but also by morals and an understanding of consequence. As such, a human being with the ability to live like a weasel has given up the very thing that makes him human.

Here, the first true flaw of Dillard's essay comes to light. While it is possible to understand and even respect Dillard's observations, it should be noted that without thought and choice she would have never been able to construct these notions in the first place. Dillard protests, "I tell you I've been in that weasel's brain for sixty seconds, and he was in mine" (Dillard 210). One cannot cast oneself into the mind of another creature without the intricacy of human thought, and one would not be able to choose to live as said creature does without the power of human choice. In essence, Dillard would not have had the ability to judge the life of another creature if she were to live like a weasel.

Comment: Again, the student acknowledges the importance of conscious thought.

Comment: While the student does not include a personal experience in the essay, this section gives us a sense of his personal view of life. Also note how he introduces the term "morals" here to point out the significance of the consequences of our actions. The point is that not only do we need to act but we also need to be aware of the result of our actions.

Comment: Student rejects Dillard's ideas but only after explaining why it is important to reject them.

Comment: Student dismantles Dillard's entire premise by telling us how the very act of writing the essay negates her argument. He has not only interpreted the essay but figured out how its premise is logically flawed.

Weasels do not make judgments; they simply act and react on the basis of instinct. The "mindlessness" that Dillard speaks of would prevent her from having the option to choose her own reactions. Whereas the conscious-thinking Dillard has the ability to see this creature and take the time to stop and examine its life, the "mindless" Dillard would only have the limited options to attack or run away. This is the major fault in the logic of Dillard's essay, as it would be impossible for her to choose to examine and compare the lives of humans and weasels without the capacity for choice.

Comment: Once again the student demonstrates why the logic of Dillard's argument falls short when applied to her own writing.

Dillard also examines a weasel's short memory in a positive light and seems to believe that a happier life could be achieved if only we were simple-minded enough to live our lives with absolutely no regret. She claims, "I suspect that for me the way is like the weasel's: open to time and death painlessly, noticing everything, remembering nothing, choosing the given with a fierce and pointed will" (Dillard 210). In theory, this does sound like a positive value. To be able to live freely without a hint of remembrance as to the results of our choices would be an interesting life, one may even say a carefree life. But at the same time, would we not be denying our responsibility as humans to learn from the mistakes of the past as to not replicate them in the future? Human beings' ability to remember is almost as important as our ability to choose, because remembering things from

Comment: This question represents excellent critical thinking. The student acknowledges that theoretically "remembering nothing" may have some merits but then ponders on the larger socio-political problem it presents.

Comment: The student brings two ideas together very smoothly here.

the past is the only way we can truly learn from them. History is taught throughout our educational system for a very good reason: so that the generations of the future do not make the mistakes of the past. A human being who chooses to live like a weasel gives up something that once made him very human: the ability to learn from his mistakes to further better himself.

Ultimately, without the ability to choose or recall the past, mankind would be able to more readily take risks without regard for consequences. Dillard views the weasel's reaction to necessity as an unwavering willingness to take such carefree risks and chances. She states that "it would be well, and proper, and obedient, and pure, to grasp your one necessity and not let it go, to dangle from it limp wherever it takes you" (Dillard 211). Would it then be productive for us to make a wrong choice and be forced to live in it forever, when we as a people have the power to change, to remedy wrongs we've made in our lives? What Dillard appears to be recommending is that humans not take many risks, but who is to say that the ability to avoid or escape risks is necessarily a flaw with mankind?

Comment: The writer sums up his argument while once again reminding us of the problem with Dillard's ideas.

Comment: This is another thoughtful question that makes the reader think along with the writer.

If we had been like the weasel, never wanting, never needing, always "choosing the given with a fierce and pointed will" (Dillard 210), our world would be a completely different place. The United States of America might not exist at this very moment if we had just taken what was given to us, and unwaveringly accepted a life as a colony of Great Britain. But as Cole clearly puts it, "A risk that you assume by actually doing something seems far more risky than a risk you take by not doing something, even though the risk of doing nothing may be greater" (Cole 145). As a unified body of people, we were able to go against that which was expected of us, evaluate the risk in doing so, and move forward with our revolution. The American people used the power of choice, and risk assessment, to make a permanent change in their lives; they used the remembrance of Britain's unjust deeds to fuel their passion for victory. We as a people chose. We remembered. We distinguished between right and wrong. These are things that a weasel can never do, because a weasel does not have a say in its own life, it only has its instincts and nothing more.

Comment: The student makes a historical reference here that serves as strong evidence for his own argument.

Humans are so unique in the fact that they can dictate the course of their own lives, but many people still choose to search around for the true way to live. What they do not realize is that they have to look no further than themselves. Our power, our weapon, is our ability to have thought and choice, to remember, and to make our own decisions based on our concepts of right and wrong, good and bad. These are the only tools we will ever need to construct the perfect life for ourselves from the ground up. And though it may seem like a nice notion to live a life free of regret, it is our responsibility as creatures and the appointed caretakers of this planet to utilize what was given to us and live our lives as we were meant to, not the life of any other wild animal.

Comment: This final paragraph sums up the writer's perspective in a thoughtful and mature way. It moves away from Dillard's argument and establishes the notion of human responsibility, an idea highly worth thinking about.

Coming to an Awareness of Language

Malcolm X

I've never been one for inaction. Everything I've ever felt strongly about, I've done something about. I guess that's why, unable to do anything else, I soon began writing to people I had known in the hustling world, such as Sammy the Pimp, John Hughes, the gambling house owner, the thief Jumpsteady, and several dope peddlers. I wrote them all about Allah and Islam and Mr. Elijah Muhammad. I had no idea where most of them lived. I addressed their letters in care of the Harlem or Roxbury bars and clubs where I'd known them.

I never got a single reply. The average hustler and criminal was too uneducated to write a letter. I have known many slick, sharp-looking hustlers, who would have you think they had an interest in Wall Street; privately, they would get someone else to read a letter if they received one. Besides, neither would I have replied to anyone writing me something as wild as "the white man is the devil."

What certainly went on the Harlem and Roxbury wires was that Detroit Red was going crazy in stir, or else he was trying some hype to shake up the warden's office.

During the years that I stayed in the Norfolk Prison Colony, never did any official directly say anything to me about those letters, although, of course, they all passed through the prison censorship. I'm sure, however, they monitored what I wrote to add to the files which every state and federal

---

prison keeps on the conversion of Negro inmates by the teachings of Mr. Elijah Muhammad.

But at that time, I felt that the real reason was that the white man knew that he was the devil.

Later on, I even wrote to the Mayor of Boston, to the Governor of Massachusetts, and to Harry S. Truman. They never answered; they probably never even saw my letters. I handscratched to them how the white man's society was responsible for the black man's condition in this wilderness of North America.

It was because of my letters that I happened to stumble upon starting to acquire some kind of a homemade education.

I became increasingly frustrated at not being able to express what I wanted to convey in letters that I wrote, especially those to Mr. Elijah Muhammad. In the street, I had been the most articulate hustler out there—I had commanded attention when I said something. But now, trying to write simple English, I not only wasn't articulate, I wasn't even functional. How would I sound writing in slang, the way I would say it, something such as, "Look, daddy, let me pull your coat about a cat, Elijah Muhammad—"

Many who today hear me somewhere in person, or on television, or those who read something I've said, will think I went to school far beyond the eighth grade. This impression is due entirely to my prison studies.

It had really begun back in the Charlestown Prison, when Bimbi first made me feel envy of his stock of knowledge. Bimbi had always taken charge of any conversation he was in, and I had tried to emulate him. But every book I picked up had few sentences which didn't contain anywhere from one to nearly all of the words that might as well have been in Chinese. When I just skipped those words, of course, I really ended up with little idea of what the book said. So I had come to the Norfolk Prison Colony still going through only book-reading motions. Pretty soon, I would have quit even these motions, unless I had received the motivation that I did.

I saw that the best thing I could do was get hold of a dictionary—to study, to learn some words. I was lucky enough to reason also that I should try to improve my penmanship. It was sad. I couldn't even write in a straight line. It was both ideas together that moved me to request a dictionary along with some tablets and pencils from the Norfolk Prison Colony school.

I spent two days just riffling uncertainly through the dictionary's pages. I'd never realized so many words existed! I didn't know which words I needed to learn. Finally, just to start some kind of action, I began copying.

In my slow, painstaking, ragged handwriting, I copied into my tablet everything printed on that first page, down to the punctuation marks.

I believe it took me a day. Then, aloud, I read back, to myself, everything I'd written on the tablet. Over and over, aloud, to myself, I read my own handwriting.

I woke up the next morning, thinking about those words—immensely proud to realize that not only had I written so much at one time, but I'd written words that I never knew were in the world. Moreover, with a little effort, I also could remember what many of these words meant. I reviewed the words whose meanings I didn't remember. Funny thing, from the dictionary first page right now, that "aardvark" springs to my mind. The dictionary had a picture of it, a long-tailed, long-eared, burrowing African mammal, which lives off termites caught by sticking out its tongue as an anteater does for ants.

I was so fascinated that I went on—I copied the dictionary's next page. And the same experience came when I studied that. With every succeeding page, I also learned of people and places and events from history. Actually the dictionary is like a miniature encyclopedia. Finally the dictionary's A section had filled a whole tablet—and I went on into the B's. That was the way I started copying what eventually became the entire dictionary. It went a lot faster after so much practice helped me to pick up handwriting speed. Between what I wrote in my tablet, and writing letters, during the rest of my time in prison I would guess I wrote a million words.

I suppose it was inevitable that as my word-base broadened, I could for the first time pick up a book and read and now begin to understand what the book was saying. Anyone who has read a great deal can imagine the new world that opened. Let me tell you something: from then until I left that prison, in every free moment I had, if I was not reading in the library, I was reading on my bunk. You couldn't have gotten me out of books with a wedge. Between Mr. Muhammad's teachings, my correspondence, my visitors . . . and my reading of books, months passed without my even thinking about being imprisoned. In fact, up to then, I never had been so truly free in my life.

How to Tame a Wild Tongue

Gloria Anzaldúa

"We're going to have to control your tongue," the dentist says, pulling out all the metal from my mouth. Silver bits plop and tinkle into the basin. My mouth is a motherlode.

The dentist is cleaning out my roots. I get a whiff of the stench when I gasp. "I can't cap that tooth yet, you're still draining," he says.

"We're going to have to do something about your tongue." I hear the anger rising in his voice. My tongue keeps pushing out the wads of cotton, pushing back the drills, the long thin needles. "I've never seen anything as strong or as stubborn," he says. And I think, how do you tame a wild tongue, train it to be quiet, how do you bridle and saddle it? How do you make it lie down?

> "Who is to say that robbing a people of its language is less violent than war?"
>
> —Ray Gwyn Smith[1]

I remember being caught speaking Spanish at recess—that was good for three licks on the knuckles with a sharp ruler. I remember being sent to the corner of the classroom for "talking back" to the Anglo teacher when all I was trying to do was tell her how to pronounce my name. "If you want to be American, speak 'American.' If you don't like it, go back to Mexico where you belong."

"I want you to speak English. *Pa' hallar buen trabajo tienes que saber hablar el inglés bien. Qué vale toda tu educación si todavía hablas inglés con un* 'accent,'" my mother would say, mortified that I spoke English like a Mexican. At Pan American University I and all Chicano students were required to take two speech classes. Their purpose: to get rid of our accents.

Attacks on one's form of expression with the intent to censor are a violation of the First Amendment. *El Anglo con cara de inocente nos arrancó la lengua.* Wild tongues can't be tamed, they can only be cut out.

OVERCOMING THE TRADITION OF SILENCE

Ahogadas, escupimos el oscuro.
Peleando con nuestra propia sombra
el silencio nos sepulta.

En boca cerrada no entran moscas. "Flies don't enter a closed mouth" is a saying I kept hearing when I was a child. *Ser habladora* was to be a gossip and a liar, to talk too much. *Muchachitas bien criadas*, well-bred girls don't answer back. *Es una falta de respeto* to talk back to one's mother or father. I remember one of the sins I'd recite to the priest in the confession box the few times I went to confession: talking back to my mother, *hablar pa' 'tras, repelar. Hocicona, repelona, chismosa*, having a big mouth, questioning, carrying tales are all signs of being *mal criada*. In my culture they are all words that are derogatory if applied to women—I've never heard them applied to men.

The first time I heard two women, a Puerto Rican and a Cuban, say the word "*nosotras*," I was shocked. I had not known the word existed. Chicanos use *nosotros* whether we're male or female. We are robbed of our female being by the masculine plural. Language is a male discourse.

And our tongues have become dry
the wilderness has dried out our tongues
and we have forgotten speech.

—Irena Klepfisz[2]

Even our own people, other Spanish speakers *nos quiren poner candados en la boca.* They would hold us back with their bag of *reglas de academia.*

Oyé como ladra: el lenguaje de la frontera

Quien tiene boca se equivoca.

—Mexican saying

"*Pocho,* cultural traitor, you're speaking the oppressor's language by speaking English, you're ruining the Spanish language," I have been accused by various Latinos and Latinas. Chicano Spanish is considered by the purist and by most Latínos deficient, a mutilation of Spanish.

But Chicano Spanish is a border tongue which developed naturally. Change, *evolución, enriquecimiento de palabras nuevas por invención o adopción* have created variants of Chicano Spanish, *un nuevo lenguaje. Un lenguaje que corresponde a un modo de vivir.* Chicano Spanish is not incorrect, it is a living language.

For a people who are neither Spanish nor live in a country in which Spanish is the first language; for a people who live in a country in which English is the reigning tongue but who are not Anglo; for a people who cannot entirely identify with either standard (formal, Castillian) Spanish nor standard English, what recourse is left to them but to create their own language? A language which they can connect their identity to, one capable of communicating the realities and values true to themselves—a language with terms that are neither *español ni inglés,* but both. We speak a patois, a forked tongue, a variation of two languages.

Chicano Spanish sprang out of the Chicanos' need to identify ourselves as a distinct people. We needed a language with which we could communicate with ourselves, a secret language. For some of us, language is a homeland closer than the Southwest—for many Chicanos today live in the Midwest and the East. And because we are a complex, heterogeneous people, we speak many languages. Some of the languages we speak are:

1. Standard English
2. Working class and slang English
3. Standard Spanish

4. Standard Mexican Spanish
5. North Mexican Spanish dialect
6. Chicano Spanish (Texas, New Mexico, Arizona, and California have regional variations)
7. Tex-Mex
8. *Pachuco* (called *caló*)

My "home" tongues are the languages I speak with my sister and brothers, with my friends. They are the last five listed, with 6 and 7 being closest to my heart. From school, the media, and job situations, I've picked up standard and working class English. From Mamagrande Locha and from reading Spanish and Mexican literature, I've picked up Standard Spanish and Standard Mexican Spanish. From *los recién llegados,* Mexican immigrants, and *braceros,* I learned the North Mexican dialect. With Mexicans I'll try to speak either Standard Mexican Spanish or the North Mexican dialect. From my parents and Chicanos living in the Valley, I picked up Chicano Texas Spanish, and I speak it with my mom, younger brother (who married a Mexican and who rarely mixes Spanish with English), aunts, and older relatives.

With Chicanas from *Nuevo México* or *Arizona* I will speak Chicano Spanish a little, but often they don't understand what I'm saying. With most California Chicanas I speak entirely in English (unless I forget). When I first moved to San Francisco, I'd rattle off something in Spanish, unintentionally embarrassing them. Often it is only with another Chicana *tejana* that I can talk freely.

Words distorted by English are known as anglicisms or *pochismos.* The *pocho* is an anglicized Mexican or American of Mexican origin who speaks Spanish with an accent characteristic of North Americans and who distorts and reconstructs the language according to the influence of English.[3] Tex-Mex, or Spanglish, comes most naturally to me. I may switch back and forth from English to Spanish in the same sentence or in the same word. With my sister and my brother Nune and with Chicano *tejano* contemporaries I speak in Tex-Mex.

From kids and people of my own age I picked up *Pachuco. Pachuco* (the language of the zoot suiters) is a language of rebellion, both against Standard

Spanish and Standard English. It is a secret language. Adults of the culture and outsiders cannot understand it. It is made up of slang words from both English and Spanish. *Ruca* means girl or woman, *vato* means guy or dude, *chale* means no, *simón* means yes, *churro* is sure, talk is *periquiar*, *pigionear* means petting, *que gacho* means how nerdy, *ponte águila* means watch out, death is called *la pelona*. Through lack of practice and not having others who can speak it, I've lost most of the *Pachuco* tongue.

CHICANO SPANISH

Chicanos, after 250 years of Spanish/Anglo colonization, have developed significant differences in the Spanish we speak. We collapse two adjacent vowels into a single syllable and sometimes shift the stress in certain words such as *maíz/maiz, cohete/cuete*. We leave out certain consonants when they appear between vowels: *lado/lao, mojado/mojao*. Chicanos from South Texas pronounce *f* as *j* as in *jue (fue)*. Chicanos use "archaisms," words that are no longer in the Spanish language, words that have been evolved out. We say *semos, truje, haiga, ansina*, and *naiden*. We retain the "archaic" *j*, as in *jalar*, that derives from an earlier *h* (the French *halar* or the Germanic *halon* which was lost to standard Spanish in the 16th century), but which is still found in several regional dialects such as the one spoken in South Texas. (Due to geography, Chicanos from the Valley of South Texas were cut off linguistically from other Spanish speakers. We tend to use words that the Spaniards brought over from Medieval Spain. The majority of the Spanish colonizers in Mexico and the Southwest came from Extremadura—Hernán Cortés was one of them—and Andalucía. Andalucians pronounce *ll* like a *y*, and their *d*'s tend to be absorbed by adjacent vowels: *tirado* becomes *tirao*. They brought *el lenguaje popular, dialectos y regionalismos.*[4])

Chicanos and other Spanish speakers also shift *ll* to *y* and *z* to *s*.[5] We leave out initial syllables, saying *tar* for *estar, toy* for *estoy, hora* for *ahora* (*cubanos* and *puertorriquenõs* also leave out initial letters of some words). We also leave out the final syllable such as *pa* for *para*. The intervocalic *y*, the *ll* as in *tortilla, ella, botella*, gets replaced by *tortia* or *tortiya, ea, botea*. We add an additional syllable at the beginning of certain words: *atocar* for *tocar, agastar* for *gastar*. Sometimes we'll say *lavaste las vacijas*, other times *lavates* (substituting the *ates* verb endings for the *aste*).

We use anglicisms, words borrowed from English: *bola* from ball, *carpeta* from carpet, *máchina de lavar* (instead of *lavadora*) from washing machine, Tex-Mex argot, created by adding a Spanish sound at the beginning or end of an English word such as *cookiar* for cook, *watchar* for watch, *parkiar* for park, and *rapiar* for rape, is the result of the pressures on Spanish speakers to adapt to English.

We don't use the word *vosotros/as* or its accompanying verb form. We don't say *claro* (to mean, yes), *imagínate*, or *me emociona*, unless we picked up Spanish from Latinas, out of a book, or in a classroom. Other Spanish-speaking groups are going through the same, or similar, development in their Spanish.

LINGUISTIC TERRORISM

Deslenguadas. Somos los del español deficiente. We are your linguistic nightmare, your linguistic aberration, your linguistic *mestisaje*, the subject of your *burla*. Because we speak with tongues of fire we are culturally crucified. Racially, culturally, and linguistically *somos huérfanos*—we speak an orphan tongue.

Chicanas who grew up speaking Chicano Spanish have internalized the belief that we speak poor Spanish. It is illegitimate, a bastard language. And because we internalize how our language has been used against us by the dominant culture, we use our language differences against each other.

Chicana feminists often skirt around each other with suspicion and hesitation. For the longest time I couldn't figure it out. Then it dawned on me. To be close to another Chicana is like looking into the mirror. We are afraid of what we'll see there. *Pena.* Shame. Low estimation of self. In childhood we are told that our language is wrong. Repeated attacks on our native tongue diminish our sense of self. The attacks continue throughout our lives.

Chicanas feel uncomfortable talking in Spanish to Latinas, afraid of their censure. Their language was not outlawed in their countries. They had a whole lifetime of being immersed in their native tongue; generations, centuries in which Spanish was a first language, taught in school, heard on radio and TV, and read in the newspaper.

If a person, Chicano or Latina, has a low estimation of my native tongue, she also has a low estimation of me. Often with *mexicanas y latinas* we'll speak English as a neutral language. Even among Chicanas we tend to speak English at parties or conferences. Yet, at the same time, we're afraid the other will think we're *agringadas* because we don't speak Chicano Spanish. We oppress each other trying to out-Chicano each other, vying to be the "real" Chicanas, to speak like Chicanos. There is no one Chicano language just as there is no one Chicano experience. A monolingual Chicana whose first language is English or Spanish is just as much a Chicana as one who speaks several variants of Spanish. A Chicana from Michigan or Chicago or Detroit is just as much a Chicana as one from the Southwest. Chicano Spanish is as diverse linguistically as it is regionally.

By the end of this century, Spanish speakers will comprise the biggest minority group in the U.S., a country where students in high schools and colleges are encouraged to take French classes because French is considered more "cultured." But for a language to remain alive it must be used.[6] By the end of this century English, and not Spanish, will be the mother tongue of most Chicanos and Latinos.

So, if you want to really hurt me, talk badly about my language. Ethnic identity is twin skin to linguistic identity—I am my language. Until I can take pride in my language, I cannot take pride in myself. Until I can accept as legitimate Chicano Texas Spanish, Tex-Mex, and all the other languages I speak, I cannot accept the legitimacy of myself. Until I am free to write bilingually and to switch codes without having always to translate, while I still have to speak English or Spanish when I would rather speak Spanglish, and as long as I have to accommodate the English speakers rather than having them accommodate me, my tongue will be illegitimate.

I will no longer be made to feel ashamed of existing. I will have my voice: Indian, Spanish, white. I will have my serpent's tongue—my woman's voice, my sexual voice, my poet's voice. I will overcome the tradition of silence.

> My fingers
> move sly against your palm
> Like women everywhere, we speak in code. . . .
>
> —Melanie Kaye/Kantrowitz[7]

"Vistas," corridos, y comida: My Native Tongue

In the 1960s, I read my first Chicano novel. It was *City of Night* by John Rechy, a gay Texan, son of a Scottish father and a Mexican mother. For days I walked around in stunned amazement that a Chicano could write and could get published. When I read *I Am Joaquín*[8] I was surprised to see a bilingual book by a Chicano in print. When I saw poetry written in Tex-Mex for the first time, a feeling of pure joy flashed through me. I felt like we really existed as a people. In 1971, when I started teaching High School English to Chicano students, I tried to supplement the required texts with works by Chicanos, only to be reprimanded and forbidden to do so by the principal. I was supposed to teach "American" and English literature. At the risk of being fired, I swore my students to secrecy and slipped in Chicano short stories, poems, a play. In graduate school, while working toward a Ph.D., I had to "argue" with one advisor after the other, semester after semester, before I was allowed to make Chicano literature an area of focus.

Even before I read books by Chicanos or Mexicans, it was the Mexican movies I saw at the drive-in—the Thursday night special of $1.00 a carload—that gave me a sense of belonging. "*Vámonos a las vistas*," my mother would call out and we'd all—grandmother, brothers, sister, and cousins—squeeze into the car. We'd wolf down cheese and bologna white bread sandwiches while watching Pedro Infante in melodramatic tearjerkers like *Nosotros los pobres*, the first "real" Mexican movie (that was not an imitation of European movie). I remember seeing *Cuando los hijos se van* and surmising that all Mexican movies played up the love a mother has for her children and what ungrateful sons and daughters suffer when they are not devoted to their mothers. I remember the singing-type "westerns" of Jorge Negrete and Miquel Aceves Mejía. When watching Mexican movies, I felt a sense of homecoming as well as alienation. People who were to amount to something didn't go to Mexican movies, or *bailes*, or tune their radios to *bolero, rancherita,* and *corrido* music.

The whole time I was growing up, there was *norteño* music sometimes called North Mexican border music, or Tex-Mex music, or Chicano music, or *cantina* (bar) music. I grew up listening to *conjuntos*, three- or four-piece bands made up of folk musicians playing guitar, *bajo sexto,* drums, and button accordion, which Chicanos had borrowed from the German immigrants who had come to Central Texas and Mexico to farm and build breweries. In the Rio Grande Valley, Steve Jordan and Little Joe Hernández were popular, and Flaco Jiménez was the accordion king. The rhythms of Tex-Mex music are those of the polka, also adapted from the Germans, who in turn had borrowed the polka from the Czechs and Bohemians.

I remember the hot, sultry evenings when *corridos*—songs of love and death on the Texas-Mexican borderlands—reverberated out of cheap amplifiers from the local *cantinas* and wafted in through my bedroom window.

Corridos first became widely used along the South Texas/Mexican border during the early conflict between Chicanos and Anglos. The *corridos* are usually about Mexican heroes who do valiant deeds against the Anglo oppressors. Pancho Villa's song, "*La cucaracha,*" is the most famous one. *Corridos* of John F. Kennedy and his death are still very popular in the Valley. Older Chicanos remember Lydia Mendoza, one of the great border *corrido* singers who was called *la Gloria de Tejas.* Her "*El tango negro,*" sung during the Great Depression, made her a singer of the people. The everpresent *corridos* narrated one hundred years of border history, bringing news of events as well as entertaining. These folk musicians and folk songs are our chief cultural mythmakers, and they made our hard lives seem bearable.

I grew up feeling ambivalent about our music. Country-western and rock-and-roll had more status. In the 50s and 60s, for the slightly educated and *agringado* Chicanos, there existed a sense of shame at being caught listening to our music. Yet I couldn't stop my feet from thumping to the music, could not stop humming the words, nor hide from myself the exhilaration I felt when I heard it.

There are more subtle ways that we internalize identification, especially in the forms of images and emotions. For me food and certain smells are tied to my identity, to my homeland. Woodsmoke curling up to an immense blue sky; woodsmoke perfuming my grandmother's clothes, her skin. The stench of cow manure and the yellow patches on the ground; the crack of a .22 rifle and the reek of cordite. Homemade white cheese sizzling in a pan, melting inside a folded *tortilla.* My sister Hilda's hot, spicy *menudo, chile colorado* making it deep red, pieces of *panza* and hominy floating on top. My brother Carito barbequing *fajitas* in the backyard. Even now and 3,000 miles away, I can see my mother spicing the ground beef, pork, and venison with *chile.* My mouth salivates at the thought of the hot steaming *tamales* I would be eating if I were home.

Si le preguntas a mi mamá, "¿Qué eres?"

"Identity is the essential core of who
we are as individuals, the conscious
experience of the self inside."

—Gershen Kaufman[9]

Nosotros los Chicanos straddle the borderlands. On one side of us, we are constantly exposed to the Spanish of the Mexicans, on the other side we hear the Anglos' incessant clamoring so that we forget our language. Among ourselves we don't say *nosotros los americanos, o nosotros los españoles, o nosotros los hispanos.* We say *nosotros los mexicanos* (by *mexicanos* we do not mean citizens of Mexico; we do not mean a national identity, but a racial one). We distinguish between *mexicanos del otro lado* and *mexicanos de este lado.* Deep in our hearts we believe that being Mexican has nothing to do with which country one lives in. Being Mexican is a state of soul—not one of mind, not one of citizenship. Neither eagle nor serpent, but both. And like the ocean, neither animal respects borders.

Dime con quien andas y te diré quien eres.
(Tell me who your friends are and I'll tell you who you are.)

—Mexican saying

Si le preguntas a mi mamá "¿Qué eres?" te dirá, "Soy mexicana." My brothers and sister say the same. I sometimes will answer "*soy mexicana*" and at others will say "*soy Chicano*" *o* "*soy tejana.*" But I identified as "*Raza*" before I ever identified as "*mexicana*" or "Chicana."

As a culture, we call ourselves Spanish when referring to ourselves as a linguistic group and when copping out. It is then that we forget our predominant Indian genes. We are 70–80 percent Indian.[10] We call ourselves Hispanic[11] or Spanish-American or Latin American or Latin when linking ourselves to other Spanish-speaking peoples of the Western hemisphere and when copping out. We call ourselves Mexican-American[12] to signify we are neither Mexican nor American, but more the noun "American" than the adjective "Mexican" (and when copping out).

Chicanos and other people of color suffer economically for not acculturating. This voluntary (yet forced) alienation makes for psychological conflict, a kind of dual identity—we don't identify with the Anglo-American cultural values and we don't totally identify with the Mexican cultural values. We are a synergy of two cultures with various degrees of Mexicanness or Angloness. I have so internalized the borderland conflict that sometimes I feel like one cancels out the other and we are zero, nothing, no one. *A veces no soy nada ni nadie. Pero hasta cuando no lo soy, lo soy.*

When not copping out, when we know we are more than nothing, we call ourselves Mexican, referring to race and ancestry; *mestizo* when affirming both our Indian and Spanish (but we hardly ever own our Black ancestory); Chicano when referring to a politically aware people born and/or raised in the U.S.; *Raza* when referring to Chicanos; *tejanos* when we are Chicanos from Texas.

Chicanos did not know we were a people until 1965 when Cesar Chavez and the farmworkers united and *I Am Joaquín* was published and *la Raza Unida* party was formed in Texas. With that recognition, we became a distinct people. Something momentous happened to the Chicano soul—we became aware of our reality and acquired a name and a language (Chicano Spanish) that reflected that reality. Now that we had a name, some of the fragmented pieces began to fall together—who we were, what we were, how we had evolved. We began to get glimpses of what we might eventually become.

Yet the struggle of identities continues, the struggle of borders is our reality still. One day the inner struggle will cease and a true integration take place. In the meantime, *tenémos que hacer la lucha. ¿Quién está protegiendo los ranchos de mi gente? ¿Quién estrá tratando de cerrar la fisura entre la india y el blanco en nuestra sangre? El Chicano, si, el Chicano que anda como un ladrón en su propia casa.*

Los Chicanos, how patient we seem, how very patient. There is the quiet of the Indian about us.[13] We know how to survive. When other races have given up their tongue, we've kept ours. We know what it is to live under the hammer blow of the dominant *norte-americano* culture. But more than we count the blows, we count the days the weeks the years the centuries the eons until the white laws and commerce and customs will rot in the deserts they've created, lie bleached. *Humildes* yet proud, *quietos* yet wild, *nosotros losmexicanos-Chicanos* will walk by the crumbling ashes as we go about our business. Stubborn, persevering, impenetrable as stone, yet possessing a malleability that renders us unbreakable, we, the *mestizas* and *mestizos,* will remain.

Notes

1. Ray Gwyn Smith, *Moorland Is Cold Country*, unpublished book.
2. Irena Klepfisz, "*Di rayze aheym*/The Journey Home," in *The Tribe of Dina: A Jewish Woman's Anthology*, Melanie Kaye/Kantrowitz and Irena Klepfisz, eds. (Montpelier, VT: Sinister Wisdom Books, 1986), 49.
3. R. C. Ortega, *Dialectología Del Barrio*, trans. Hortencia S. Alwan (Los Angeles, CA: R. C. Ortega Publisher & Bookseller, 1977), 132.
4. Eduardo Hernandéz-Chávez, Andrew D. Cohen, and Anthony F. Beltramo, *El Lenguaje de los Chicanos: Regional and Social Characteristics of Language Used by Mexican Americans* (Arlington, VA: Center for Applied Linguistics, 1975), 39.
5. Hernandéz-Chávez, xvii.
6. Irena Klepfisz, "Secular Jewish Identity: Yidishkayt in America," in *The Tribe of Dina*, Kaye/Kantrowitz and Klepfisz, eds., 43.
7. Melanie Kaye/Kantrowitz, "Sign," in *We Speak in Code: Poems and Other Writings* (Pittsburgh, PA: Motheroot Publications, Inc., 1980), 85.
8. Rodolfo Gonzales, *I Am Joaquín/Yo Soy Joaquín* (New York, NY: Bantam Books, 1972). It was first published in 1967.
9. Gershen Kaufman, *Shame: The Power of Caring* (Cambridge, MA: Schenkman Books, Inc., 1980), 68.
10. John R. Chávez, *The Lost Land: The Chicago Images of the Southwest* (Albuquerque, NM: University of New Mexico Press, 1984), 88–90.
11. "Hispanic" is derived from *Hispanis (España*, a name given to the Iberian Peninsula in ancient times when it was a part of the Roman Empire) and is a term designated by the U.S. government to make it easier to handle us on paper.
12. The Treaty of Guadalupe Hidalgo created the Mexican-American in 1848.
13. Anglos, in order to alleviate their guilt for dispossessing the Chicano, stressed the Spanish part of us and perpetrated the myth of the Spanish Southwest. We have accepted the fiction that we are Hispanic, that is Spanish, in order to accommodate ourselves to the dominant culture and its abhorrence of Indians. Chávez, 88–91.

Bowman 1

Nicole Bowman

Anne Wheeler

College Writing 113-16

September 29, 2015

What a Nun Taught Me About Feminism

At 9:47 am on August 27th, 2015, the door to a new world of literacy was cracked open. It was the first day of my senior year in high school. I strolled into room 36 that morning sporting my senior blue tie dye and a smile that was far too big for my face. It was time for the Bay View Academy students to start their period B class. No other girl in Mercy Hall would be as happy as I was during those ninety minutes in our academic schedules. This was not just any class; this was Honors Literary Analysis with Sister Carol.

Sister Carol is not your run of the mill nun. She does not wear a habit or smack our knuckles with rulers. No, Sister Carol is a Sister of Mercy, the cool order of nuns. She is a kind, selfless, and intelligent teacher who was not afraid to touch upon controversial topics. With her profound voice, glasses, blonde pixie haircut, and fabulous sass, she ran the classroom like no one's business. Sister Carol incorporated major political and ethical themes and issues throughout our course's curriculum that challenged us not just as students, but as human beings. Her lessons and assignments made me ask myself what it means to be a woman in our world. Sister Carol's class made me the feminist I am today, and for that I am truly grateful.

I took a seat at an open desk. After some brief introductions and an overview of the syllabus, the first lesson began. "Literature is art, Ladies." Sister Carol summed up the beautiful system of written words so simply. She continued with her lecture, "literature uses words to unleash creativity, self-expression, and emotion, much like any art piece." But how do we as readers tap into that? Sister Carol explained how writers use diction, syntax, tone, and imagery to paint their masterpieces.

This new vocabulary awakened the reader in me that always wanted more. We learned how writers do not choose their words willy-nilly. A writer thinks about what they want to say and that is the unique pattern of language they choose. No other person on this earth would write the same exact piece. We learned to listen and feel the atmosphere the writing gave us. Is it creepy and haunting? Motivational and uplifting? Humorous and entertaining? Boring and dull? We learned to be attentive to the images and figurative language the author provides. The writer is painting you a picture and it is necessary to look at it to understand the artwork.

Sister Carol equipped us with our annotation toolbox on the first day of class. That has been the greatest gift I have received in high school. I now had the ability to connect to a world that I thought I knew, but had no idea how truly amazing it really was. It was time to explore. We were going to be digging deep into literature and getting dirty with words.

Our very first assignment was to read and annotate an essay entitled, "Wholeness," written by Joan Chittister. We were to highlight vivid imagery, figures of speech, and note words or phrases that had meaning to us. I had never done something like this before. I never thought about what was behind the words, all my life I was only touching the surface. Now I was probing, picking, and pulling apart every syllable of an essay.

Using my fancy Notability App on my iPad, I underlined, highlighted, and made notes all over the pages. My screen became a rainbow of literary analysis. I was really tuning into the words, content, and the voice of Joan

Chittister. Paying close attention to the figurative language and reason behind the writing made me feel Chittister's fiery spirit. She blended ecology, theology, feminism so beautifully into a new worldview. Her essay was focused on how humans have turned away from God, exploited all of Mother Earth's resources, and are treating women like "potted plants." She listed ten ideals that humanity has created and lives because we believe that "each plane of creation is higher than the last." Humanity has molded all of the earth's creation into a pyramid of power. Joan sarcastically states, "humans are superior to nature, and men – males – the crown, the pinnacle, the divine pride of creation, are superior to women." Underneath the top tiers of humanity are all of our resources. Men come to believe that "nature has no reason for existence except to serve human existence." The men suppress the power and importance of God, women, and nature all throughout time. If you think Chittister is making this up, please, open a history book.

Joan Chittister proposed a new worldview. One in which we see God, men, women, and the environment as one, a "concert of waves." She explains that, "Eco-feminism brings humanity to wholeness, wholeness to religion, and integrity to a science, which having proved that there is no one species on earth that is the only one that counts, does, in that instance, give the lie to the anthropocentric to the andocentric, and to the oppression and invisibility in the public arena of women as well." This woman quickly became my eco-feminism superhero.

"Wholeness" taught me that feminism is multidimensional. We have a big issue on our hands. Women are fighting the "crown of creation" for equality and autonomy, but what are we going to do with those once we

Bowman 4

get it? How are we going to tell the male species that their worldview is totally wrong and we need to fix it? We need to unleash the power of eco-feminism. Peace comes when we see all creation as extension of life. Every race, species, planet, body of water, needs to be treated with respect and love because we were all created by one God. There is one spirit that lives in all, all of earth is really one body. Treating women poorly is like punching yourself in stomach; your whole body is going to ache if you do not stop. A healthy body needs holistic love and care, and so does creation.

"Wholeness," was an excellent introduction to our very first unit in the course, "Women's Struggle for Self-Realization." We read and annotated a number or essays, short stories, plays, and a novel. These selections included *A Doll's House*, "Chrysanthemums," "Miss Brill," and "Eveline." Each story shouted feminism louder and louder as I became better at annotating and analyzing.

The independent reading selection for this unit was *Handmaid's Tale*, by Margaret Atwood. The novel is set in a fictional future when human reproduction becomes extremely difficult due to the high population of "sterile" men in America. The government takes control in the epidemic. Guards invade every home and take all the women away to prepare them for their mission in this new society, The Republic of Gilead. Each woman is given their own job: Martha, Aunt, or handmaid. The main character, Offred, is torn away from her husband and daughter to become the handmaid to "The Commander". The Republic of Gilead is a nation of no humanity, no love, and absolutely no autonomy.

As a handmaid, Offred is responsible for human reproduction in Gilead. One certain nights, she must participate in what is called, "the ceremony." During this event, Offred engages in sexual intercourse with The Commander while she lies down in his wife's lap. This is to symbolize that the two women are one. There is absolutely nothing pleasurable about "the ceremony." All three participants hate it. Atwood is trying to make a point through this very weird scene that women are nothing but containers in society. Their reason for being is solely biological, to conceive, carry, and give birth to a child so the human species does not become extinct.

Along with reading this complex novel and writing a paper, an entire class period was dedicated to discussing the novel in a seminar. Sister Carol initiated the seminar by asking us what we liked and did not like about the book. I assure you, no other girl in my class has ever read a novel similar to *Handmaid's Tale.* This made our very first independent reading seminar all the more awkward. The classroom fell silent. The novel had some very graphic sexual scenes, which was the big elephant in the room.

Sister Carol is not a conventional Catholic nun; she was completely comfortable with talking about sex. Ironically, a group of teenagers were the ones having trouble talking about such topics. She whipped out her incredible sass and started referring to sex as "tumbling." I love how Sister Carol used her spunky personality to break the ice. As the seminar progressed, we became more comfortable talking about the novel with our classmates. The conversation quickly escalated when we discussed our hatred for The Commander and our love for Nick, a Gilead guard. Themes such as feminism, autonomy, freedom, and the potential of women were examined and debated. We ended the conversation by talking about how this book is relevant in our society and the world today. My own opinion, which was shared by many of my classmates, was that women everywhere are being degraded to housewives, caregivers, and baby makers when we have so much more to offer. Both males and females are blind to the amazing abilities women have.

This seminar enhanced my literary understanding because I could talk intelligibly about my understandings of the novel and listen to the interpretations of others. "Women's Struggle for Self-Realization" allowed feminism to grab my hand and pull me into the pages. I danced along the lines of essays, plays, and books with a new understanding of what it is to read.

I grew in my literacy every day senior year. I was analyzing the words intensely, understanding complex themes clearly, making connection between my own life experiences and what I was reading, and feeling the writer's emotions more deeply. Before Sister Carol's class, literature was a square. Now it is a box. I never knew I could I pick it up, turn it over, open it up, and unpack what is inside.

PART 2

Engaging With Texts

How to Read Like a Writer

Mike Bunn

In 1997, I was a recent college graduate living in London for six months and working at the Palace Theatre owned by Andrew Lloyd Webber.* The Palace was a beautiful red brick, four-story theatre in the heart of London's famous West End, and eight times a week it housed a three-hour performance of the musical *Les Miserables.* Because of antiquated fire-safety laws, every theatre in the city was required to have a certain number of staff members inside watching the performance in case of an emergency.

My job (in addition to wearing a red tuxedo jacket) was to sit inside the dark theater with the patrons and make sure nothing went wrong. It didn't seem to matter to my supervisor that I had no training in security and no idea where we kept the fire extinguishers. I was pretty sure that if there *was* any trouble I'd be running down the back stairs, leaving the patrons to fend for themselves. I had no intention of dying in a bright red tuxedo.

There was a Red Coat stationed on each of the theater's four floors, and we all passed the time by sitting quietly in the back, reading books with tiny flashlights. It's not easy trying to read in the dim light of a theatre—flashlight or no flashlight—and it's even tougher with shrieks and shouts and gunshots coming from the stage. I had to focus intently on each and every word, often rereading a single sentence several times. Sometimes I got distracted and had to re-read entire paragraphs. As I struggled to read in this environment, I began to realize that the way I was reading—one word at a time—was exactly the same way that the author had written the text. I realized writing is a word-by-word, sentence-by-sentence process. The intense concentration required to read in the theater helped me recognize some of the interesting ways that authors string words into phrases into paragraphs into entire books.

I came to realize that all writing consists of a series of choices.

I was an English major in college, but I don't think I ever thought much about reading. I read all the time. I read for my classes and on the computer and sometimes for fun, but I never really thought about the important connections between reading and writing, and how reading in a particular way could also make me a better writer.

WHAT DOES IT MEAN TO READ LIKE A WRITER?

When you Read Like a Writer (*RLW*) you work to identify some of the choices the author made so that you can better understand how such choices might arise in your own writing. The idea is to carefully examine the things you read, looking at the writerly techniques in the text in order to decide if you might want to adopt similar (or the same) techniques in your writing.

You are reading to learn about writing.

Instead of reading for content or to better understand the ideas in the writing (which you will automatically do to some degree anyway), you are trying to understand how the piece of writing was put together by the author and what you can learn about writing by reading a particular text. As you read in this way, you think about how the choices the author made and the techniques that he/she used are influencing your own responses as a reader. What is it about the way this text is written that makes you feel and respond the way you do?

The goal as you read like a writer is to locate what you believe are the most important writerly choices represented in the text—choices as large as the overall structure or as small as a single word used only once—to consider the effect of those choices on potential readers (including yourself). Then you can go one step further and imagine what *different* choices the author *might* have made instead, and what effect those different choices would have on readers.

Say you're reading an essay in class that begins with a short quote from President Barack Obama about the war in Iraq. As a writer, what do you think of this technique? Do you think it is effective to begin the essay with a quote? What if the essay began with a quote from someone else? What if it was a much *longer* quote from President Obama, or a quote from the President about something other than the war?

And here is where we get to the most important part: *Would you want to try this technique in your own writing?*

Would you want to start your own essay with a quote? Do you think it would be effective to begin your essay with a quote from President Obama? What about a quote from someone else?

You could make yourself a list. What are the advantages and disadvantages of starting with a quote? What about the advantages and disadvantages of starting with a quote from the President? How would other readers respond to this technique? Would certain readers (say Democrats or liberals) appreciate an essay that started with a quote from President Obama better than other readers (say Republicans or conservatives)? What would be the advantages and disadvantages of starting with a quote from a *less* divisive person? What about starting with a quote from someone *more* divisive?

The goal is to carefully consider the choices the author made and the techniques that he or she used, and then decide whether you want to make those same choices or use those same techniques in your own writing. Author and professor Wendy Bishop explains how her reading process changed when she began to read like a writer:

> It wasn't until I claimed the sentence as my area of desire, interest, and expertise—until I wanted to be a writer writing better—that I had to look underneath my initial readings . . . I started asking, *how—how* did the writer get me to feel, *how* did the writer say something so that it remains in my memory when many other things too easily fall out, *how* did the writer communicate his/her intentions about genre, about irony? (119–20)

Bishop moved from simply reporting her personal reactions to the things she read to attempting to uncover *how* the author led her (and other readers) to have those reactions. This effort to uncover how authors build texts is what makes *Reading Like a Writer* so useful for student writers.

HOW IS *RLW* DIFFERENT FROM "NORMAL" READING?

Most of the time we read for information. We read a recipe to learn how to bake lasagna. We read the sports page to see if our school won the game, Facebook to see who has commented on our status update, a history book to learn about the Vietnam War, and the syllabus to see when the next writing assignment is due. *Reading Like a Writer* asks for something very different.

In 1940, a famous poet and critic named Allen Tate discussed two different ways of reading:

> There are many ways to read, but generally speaking there are two ways. They correspond to the two ways in which we may be interested in a piece of architecture. If the building has Corinthian columns, we can trace the origin and development of Corinthian columns; we are interested as historians. But if we are interested as architects, we may or may not know about the history of the Corinthian style; we must, however, know all about the construction of the building, down to the last nail or peg in the beams. We have got to know this if we are going to put up buildings ourselves. (506)

While I don't know anything about Corinthian columns (and doubt that I will ever *want* to know anything about Corinthian columns), Allen Tate's metaphor of reading as if you were an architect is a great way to think about

RLW. When you read like a writer, you are trying to figure out how the text you are reading was constructed so that you learn how to "build" one for yourself. Author David Jauss makes a similar comparison when he writes that "reading won't help you much unless you learn to read like a writer. You must look at a book the way a carpenter looks at a house someone else built, examining the details in order to see how it was made" (64).

Perhaps I should change the name and call this Reading Like an Architect, or Reading Like a Carpenter. In a way those names make perfect sense. You are reading to see how something was constructed so that you can construct something similar yourself.

WHY LEARN TO READ LIKE A WRITER?

For most college students *RLW* is a new way to read, and it can be difficult to learn at first. Making things even *more* difficult is that your college writing instructor may expect you to read this way for class but never actually teach you how to do it. He or she may not even tell you that you're supposed to read this way. This is because most writing instructors are so focused on teaching writing that they forget to show students how they want them to read.

That's what this essay is for.

In addition to the fact that your college writing instructor may expect you to read like a writer, this kind of reading is also one of the very best ways to learn how to write well. Reading like a writer can help you understand how the process of writing is a series of making choices, and in doing so, can help you recognize important decisions you might face and techniques you might want to use when working on your own writing. Reading this way becomes an opportunity to think and learn about writing.

Charles Moran, a professor of English at the University of Massachusetts, urges us to read like writers because:

> When we read like writers we understand and participate in the writing. We see the choices the writer has made, and we see how the writer has coped with the consequences of those choices . . . We "see" what the writer is doing because we read as writers; we see because

> we have written ourselves and know the territory, know the feel of it, know some of the moves ourselves. (61)

You are already an author, and that means you have a built-in advantage when reading like a writer. All of your previous writing experiences—inside the classroom and out—can contribute to your success with *RLW*. Because you "have written" things yourself, just as Moran suggests, you are better able to "see" the choices that the author is making in the texts that you read. This in turn helps you to think about whether you want to make some of those same choices in your own writing, and what the consequences might be for your readers if you do.

WHAT ARE SOME QUESTIONS TO ASK BEFORE YOU START READING?

As I sat down to work on this essay, I contacted a few of my former students to ask what advice they would give to college students regarding how to read effectively in the writing classroom and also to get their thoughts on *RLW*. Throughout the rest of the essay I'd like to share some of their insights and suggestions; after all, who is better qualified to help you learn what you need to know about reading in college writing courses than students who recently took those courses themselves?

One of the things that several students mentioned to do first, before you even start reading, is to consider the *context* surrounding both the assignment and the text you're reading. As one former student, Alison, states: "The reading I did in college asked me to go above and beyond, not only in breadth of subject matter, but in depth, with regards to informed analysis and background information on *context*." Alison was asked to think about some of the factors that went into the creation of the text, as well as some of the factors influencing her own experience of reading—taken together these constitute the *context* of reading. Another former student, Jamie, suggests that students "learn about the historical context of the writings" they will read for class. Writing professor Richard Straub puts it this way: "You're not going to just read a text. You're going to read a text within a certain context, a set of circumstances . . . It's one kind of writing or another, designed for one audience and purpose or another" (138).

Among the contextual factors you'll want to consider before you even start reading are:

- Do you know the author's purpose for this piece of writing?
- Do you know who the intended audience is for this piece of writing?

It may be that you need to start reading before you can answer these first two questions, but it's worth trying to answer them before you start. For example, if you know at the outset that the author is trying to reach a very specific group of readers, then his or her writerly techniques may seem more or less effective than if he/she was trying to reach a more general audience. Similarly—returning to our earlier example of beginning an essay with a quote from President Obama about the war in Iraq—if you know that the author's purpose is to address some of the dangers and drawbacks of warfare, this may be a very effective opening. If the purpose is to encourage Americans to wear sunscreen while at the beach this opening makes no sense at all. One former student, Lola, explained that most of her reading assignments in college writing classes were designed "to provoke analysis and criticisms into the style, structure, and *purpose* of the writing itself."

IN WHAT GENRE IS THIS WRITTEN?

Another important thing to consider before reading is the genre of the text. Genre means a few different things in college English classes, but it's most often used to indicate the *type* of writing: a poem, a newspaper article, an essay, a short story, a novel, a legal brief, an instruction manual, etc. Because the conventions for each genre can be very different (who ever heard of a 900-page newspaper article?), techniques that are effective for one genre may not work well in another. Many readers expect poems and pop songs to rhyme, for example, but might react negatively to a legal brief or instruction manual that did so.

Another former student, Mike, comments on how important the genre of the text can be for reading:

> I think a lot of the way I read, of course, depends on the type of text I'm reading. If I'm reading philosophy, I always look for signaling

> words (however, therefore, furthermore, despite) indicating the direction of the argument . . . when I read fiction or creative nonfiction, I look for how the author inserts dialogue or character sketches within narration or environmental observation. After reading To the Lighthouse [sic] last semester, I have noticed how much more attentive I've become to the types of narration (omniscient, impersonal, psychological, realistic, etc.), and how these different approaches are utilized to achieve an author's overall effect.

Although Mike specifically mentions what he looked for while reading a published novel, one of the great things about *RLW* is that it can be used equally well with either published or student-produced writing.

IS THIS A PUBLISHED OR A STUDENT-PRODUCED PIECE OF WRITING?

As you read both kinds of texts you can locate the choices the author made and imagine the different decisions that he/she might have made.

While it might seem a little weird at first to imagine how published texts could be written differently—after all, they were good enough to be published—remember that all writing can be improved. Scholar Nancy Walker believes that it's important for students to read published work using *RLW* because "the work ceases to be a mere artifact, a stone tablet, and becomes instead a living utterance with immediacy and texture. It could have been better or worse than it is had the author made different choices" (36). As Walker suggests, it's worth thinking about how the published text would be different—maybe even *better*—if the author had made different choices in the writing because you may be faced with similar choices in your own work.

IS THIS THE KIND OF WRITING YOU WILL BE ASSIGNED TO WRITE YOURSELF?

Knowing ahead of time what kind of writing assignments you will be asked to complete can really help you to read like a writer. It's probably impossible (and definitely too time-consuming) to identify *all* of the choices the author made and *all* techniques an author used, so it's important to prioritize while reading. Knowing what you'll be writing yourself can help you prioritize. It may be the case that your instructor has assigned the text you're reading to serve as a model for the kind of writing you'll be doing later. Jessie, a former student, writes, "In college writing classes, we knew we were reading for a purpose—to influence or inspire our own work. The reading that I have done in college writing courses has always been really specific to a certain type of writing, and it allows me to focus and experiment on that specific style in depth and without distraction."

If the text you're reading is a model of a particular style of writing—for example, highly-emotional or humorous—*RLW* is particularly helpful because you can look at a piece you're reading and think about whether you want to adopt a similar style in your own writing. You might realize that the author is trying to arouse sympathy in readers and examine what techniques he/she uses to do this; then you can decide whether these techniques might work well in your own writing. You might notice that the author keeps including jokes or funny stories and think about whether you want to include them in your writing—what would the impact be on your potential readers?

WHAT ARE QUESTIONS TO ASK AS YOU ARE READING?

It is helpful to continue to ask yourself questions *as* you read like a writer. As you're first learning to read in this new way, you may want to have a set of questions written or typed out in front of you that you can refer to while reading. Eventually—after plenty of practice—you will start to ask certain questions and locate certain things in the text almost automatically. Remember, for most students this is a new way of reading, and you'll have to train yourself to do it well. Also keep in mind that you're reading to understand how the text was *written*—how the house was built—more than you're trying to determine the meaning of the things you read or assess whether the texts are good or bad.

First, return to two of the same questions I suggested that you consider *before* reading:

- What is the author's purpose for this piece of writing?
- Who is the intended audience?

Think about these two questions again as you read. It may be that you couldn't really answer them before, or that your ideas will change while reading. Knowing *why* the piece was written and *who* it's for can help explain why the author might have made certain choices or used particular techniques in the writing, and you can assess those choices and techniques based in part on how effective they are in fulfilling that purpose and/or reaching the intended audience.

Beyond these initial two questions, there is an almost endless list of questions you might ask regarding writing choices and techniques. Here are some of the questions that one former student, Clare, asks herself:

> When reading I tend to be asking myself a million questions. If I were writing this, where would I go with the story? If the author goes in a different direction (as they so often do) from what I am thinking, I will ask myself, why did they do this? What are they telling me?

Clare tries to figure out why the author might have made a move in the writing that she hadn't anticipated, but even more importantly, she asks herself what *she* would do if she were the author. Reading the text becomes an opportunity for Clare to think about her own role as an author.

Here are some additional examples of the kinds of questions you might ask yourself as you read:

- How effective is the language the author uses? Is it too formal? Too informal? Perfectly appropriate?

Depending on the subject matter and the intended audience, it may make sense to be more or less formal in terms of language. As you begin reading, you can ask yourself whether the word choice and tone/language of the writing seem appropriate.

- What kinds of evidence does the author use to support his/her claims? Does he/she use statistics? Quotes from famous people? Personal anecdotes or personal stories? Does he/she cite books or articles?
- How appropriate or effective is this evidence? Would a different type of evidence, or some combination of evidence, be more effective?

To some extent the kinds of questions you ask should be determined by the genre of writing you are reading. For example, it's probably worth examining the evidence that the author uses to support his/ her claims if you're reading an opinion column, but less important if you're reading a short story. An opinion column is often intended to convince readers of something, so the kinds of evidence used are often very important. A short story *may* be intended to convince readers of something, sometimes, but probably not in the same way. A short story rarely includes claims or evidence in the way that we usually think about them.

- Are there places in the writing that you find confusing? What about the writing in those places makes it unclear or confusing?

It's pretty normal to get confused in places while reading, especially while reading for class, so it can be helpful to look closely at the writing to try and get a sense of exactly what tripped you up. This way you can learn to avoid those same problems in your own writing.

- How does the author move from one idea to another in the writing? Are the transitions between the ideas effective? How else might he/she have transitioned between ideas instead?

Notice that in these questions I am encouraging you to question whether aspects of the writing are *appropriate* and *effective* in addition to deciding whether you liked or disliked them. You want to imagine how other readers might respond to the writing and the techniques you've identified. Deciding whether you liked or disliked something is only about you; considering whether a technique is appropriate or effective lets you contemplate what the author might have been trying to do and to decide whether a majority of readers would find the move successful. This is important because it's the same thing you should be thinking about while you are writing: how will readers respond to this technique I am using, to this sentence, to this word? As you read, ask yourself what the author is doing at each step of the way, and then consider whether the same choice or technique might work in your own writing.

WHAT SHOULD YOU BE WRITING AS YOU ARE READING?

The most common suggestion made by former students—mentioned by every single one of them—was to mark up the text, make comments in the margins, and write yourself notes and summaries both during and after reading. Often the notes students took while reading became ideas or material for the students to use in their own papers. It's important to read with a pen or highlighter in your hand so that you can mark—right on the text—all those spots where you identify an interesting choice the author has made or a writerly technique you might want to use. One thing that I like to do is to highlight and underline the passage in the text itself, and then try to answer the following three questions on my notepad:

- What is the technique the author is using here?
- Is this technique effective?
- What would be the advantages and disadvantages if I tried this same technique in my writing?

By utilizing this same process of highlighting and note taking, you'll end up with a useful list of specific techniques to have at your disposal when it comes time to begin your own writing.

WHAT DOES *RLW* LOOK LIKE IN ACTION?

Let's go back to the opening paragraph of *this* essay and spend some time reading like writers as a way to get more comfortable with the process:

> *In 1997, I was a recent college graduate living in London for six months and working at the Palace Theatre owned by Andrew Lloyd Webber. The Palace was a beautiful red brick, four-story theatre in the heart of London's famous West End, and eight times a week it housed a three-hour performance of the musical* Les Miserables. *Because of antiquated fire-safety laws, every theatre in the city was required to have a certain number of staff members inside watching the performance in case of an emergency.*

Let's begin with those questions I encouraged you to try to answer *before* you start reading. (I realize we're cheating a little bit in this case since you've already read most of this essay, but this is just practice. When doing this on your own, you should attempt to answer these questions before reading, and then return to them as you read to further develop your answers.)

- Do you know the author's purpose for this piece of writing? I hope the purpose is clear by now; if it isn't, I'm doing a pretty lousy job of explaining how and why you might read like a writer.
- Do you know who the intended audience is? Again, I hope that you know this one by now.
- What about the genre? Is this an essay? An article? What would *you* call it?
- You know that it's published and not student writing. How does this influence your expectations for what you will read?
- Are you going to be asked to write something like this yourself? Probably not in your college writing class, but you can still use *RLW* to learn about writerly techniques that you might want to use in whatever you do end up writing.

Now ask yourself questions *as* you read.

> *In 1997, I was a recent college graduate living in London for six months and working at the Palace Theatre owned by Andrew Lloyd Webber. The Palace was a beautiful red brick, four-story theatre in the heart of London's famous West End, and eight times a week it housed a three-hour performance of the musical* Les Miserables. *Because of antiquated fire-safety laws, every theatre in the city was required to have a certain number of staff members inside watching the performance in case of an emergency.*

Since this paragraph is the very first one, it makes sense to think about how it introduces readers to the essay. What technique(s) does the author use to begin the text? This is a personal story about his time working in London. What else do you notice as you read over this passage? Is the passage vague or specific about where he worked? You know that the author worked in a famous part of London in a beautiful theater owned by a well-known composer. Are these details important? How different would this opening be if instead I had written:

> *In 1997, I was living in London and working at a theatre that showed* Les Miserables.

This is certainly shorter, and some of you may prefer this version. It's quick. To the point. But what (if anything) is lost by eliminating so much of the detail? I *chose* to include each of the details that the revised sentence omits, so it's worth considering why. Why did I mention where the theater was located? Why did I explain that I was living in London right after finishing college? Does it matter that it was after college? What effect might I have hoped the inclusion of these details would have on readers? Is this reference to college an attempt to connect with my audience of college students? Am I trying to establish my credibility as an author by announcing that I went to college? Why might I want the readers to know that this was a theater owned by Andrew Lloyd Weber? Do you think I am just trying to mention a famous name that readers will recognize? Will Andrew Lloyd Webber figure prominently in the rest of the essay?

These are all reasonable questions to ask. They are not necessarily the *right* questions to ask because there are no right questions. They certainly aren't the only questions you could ask, either. The goal is to train yourself to formulate questions as you read based on whatever you notice in the text. Your own reactions to what you're reading will help determine the kinds of questions to ask.

Now take a broader perspective. I begin this essay—an essay about *reading*—by talking about my job in a theater in London. Why? Doesn't this seem like an odd way to begin an essay about reading? If you read on a little further (feel free to scan back up at the top of this essay) you learn in the third full paragraph what the connection is between working in the theater and reading like a writer, but why include this information at all? What does this story add to the essay? Is it worth the space it takes up?

Think about what effect presenting this personal information might have on readers. Does it make it feel like a real person, some "ordinary guy," is talking to you? Does it draw you into the essay and make you want to keep reading?

What about the language I use? Is it formal or more informal? This is a time when you can really narrow your focus and look at particular words:

> *Because of antiquated fire-safety laws, every theatre in the city was required to have a certain number of staff members inside watching the performance in case of an emergency.*

What is the effect of using the word "antiquated" to describe the fire-safety laws? It certainly projects a negative impression; if the laws are described as antiquated it means I view them as old-fashioned or obsolete. This is a fairly uncommon word, so it stands out, drawing attention to my choice in using it. The word also sounds quite formal. Am I formal in the rest of this sentence?

I use the word "performance" when I just as easily could have written "show." For that matter, I could have written "old" instead of "antiquated." You can proceed like this throughout the sentence, thinking about alternative choices I could have made and what the effect would be. Instead of "staff members" I could have written "employees" or just "workers." Notice the difference if the sentence had been written:

> *Because of old fire-safety laws, every theatre in the city was required to have a certain number of workers inside watching the show in case of an emergency.*

Which version is more likely to appeal to readers? You can try to answer this question by thinking about the advantages and disadvantages of using formal language. When would you want to use formal language in your writing and when would it make more sense to be more conversational?

As you can see from discussing just this one paragraph, you could ask questions about the text forever. Luckily, you don't have to. As you continue reading like a writer, you'll learn to notice techniques that seem new and pay less attention to the ones you've thought about before. The more you practice the quicker the process becomes until you're reading like a writer almost automatically.

I want to end this essay by sharing one more set of comments by my former student, Lola, this time about what it means to her to read like a writer:

> Reading as a writer would compel me to question what might have brought the author to make these decisions, and then decide what worked and what didn't. What could have made that chapter better or easier to understand? How can I make sure I include some of the good attributes of this writing style into my own? How can I take aspects that I feel the writer failed at and make sure not to make the same mistakes in my writing?

Questioning why the author made certain decisions. Considering what techniques could have made the text better. Deciding how to include the best attributes of what you read in your own writing. This is what *Reading Like a Writer* is all about.

Are you ready to start reading?

Works Cited

Bishop, Wendy. "Reading, Stealing, and Writing Like a Writer." *Elements of Alternate Style: Essays on Writing and Revision.* Ed. Wendy Bishop. Portsmouth, NH: Boynton/Cook, 1997. Print.

Jauss, David. "Articles of Faith." *Creative Writing in America: Theory and Pedagogy.* Ed. Joseph Moxley. Urbana, IL: NCTE, 1989. Print.

Moran, Charles. "Reading Like a Writer." *Vital Signs 1.* Ed. James L. Collins. Portsmouth, NH: Boynton/Cook, 1990. Print.

Straub, Richard. "Responding—Really Responding—to Other Students' Writing." *The Subject is Reading.* Ed. Wendy Bishop. Portsmouth, NH: Boynton/Cook, 2000. Print.

Tate, Allen. "We Read as Writers." *Princeton Alumni Weekly* 40 (March 8, 1940): 505–506. Print.

Walker, Nancy. "The Student Reader as Writer." *ADE Bulletin* 106 (1993): 35–37. Print.

Burke's "Unending Conversation" Metaphor

Kenneth Burke writes:

Imagine that you enter a parlor. You come late. When you arrive, others have long preceded you, and they are engaged in a heated discussion, a discussion too heated for them to pause and tell you exactly what it is about. In fact, the discussion had already begun long before any of them got there, so that no one present is qualified to retrace for you all the steps that had gone before. You listen for a while, until you decide that you have caught the tenor of the argument; then you put in your oar. Someone answers; you answer him; another comes to your defense; another aligns himself against you, to either the embarrassment or gratification of your opponent, depending upon the quality of your ally's assistance. However, the discussion is interminable. The hour grows late, you must depart. And you do depart, with the discussion still vigorously in progress.

From *The Philosophy of Literary Form*, pp. 110–111.

Explaining White Privilege to a Broke White Person

Gina Crosley-Corcoran

Years ago some feminist on the Internet told me I was "privileged."

"THE F&CK!?!?" I said.

I came from the kind of poor that people don't want to believe still exists in this country. Have you ever spent a frigid northern-Illinois winter without heat or running water? I have. At 12 years old were you making ramen noodles in a coffee maker with water you fetched from a public bathroom? I was. Have you ever lived in a camper year-round and used a random relative's apartment as your mailing address? We did. Did you attend so many different elementary schools that you can only remember a quarter of their names? Welcome to my childhood.

This is actually a much nicer trailer setup than the one I grew up in.

So when that feminist told me I had "white privilege," I told her that my white skin didn't do shit to prevent me from experiencing poverty. Then, like any good, educated feminist would, she directed me to Peggy McIntosh's now-famous 1988 piece "White Privilege: Unpacking the Invisible Knapsack."

After one reads McIntosh's powerful essay, it's impossible to deny that being born with white skin in America affords people certain unearned privileges in life that people of other skin colors simply are not afforded. For example:

"I can turn on the television or open to the front page of the paper and see people of my race widely represented."

"When I am told about our national heritage or about 'civilization,' I am shown that people of my color made it what it is."

"If a traffic cop pulls me over or if the IRS audits my tax return, I can be sure I haven't been singled out because of my race."

"I can if I wish arrange to be in the company of people of my race most of the time."

If you read through the rest of the list, you can see how white people and people of color experience the world in very different ways. But listen: This is not said to make white people feel guilty about their privilege. It's not your fault that you were born with white skin and experience these privileges. But whether you realize it or not, you *do* benefit from it, and it *is* your fault if you don't maintain awareness of that fact.

I do understand that McIntosh's essay may rub some people the wrong way. There are several points on the list that I felt spoke more to the author's status as a middle-class person than to her status as a white person. For example:

"If I should need to move, I can be pretty sure of renting or purchasing housing in an area, which I can afford and in which I would want to live."

"I can be pretty sure that my neighbors in such a location will be neutral or pleasant to me."

"I can go shopping alone most of the time, pretty well assured that I will not be followed or harassed."

"If I want to, I can be pretty sure of finding a publisher for this piece on white privilege."

And there are so many more points in the essay where the word "class" could be substituted for the word "race," which would ultimately paint a very different picture. That is why I had such a hard time identifying with this essay for so long. When I first wrote about white privilege years ago, I demanded to know why this white woman felt that my experiences were the same as hers when, no, my family most certainly could not rent housing "in an area which we could afford and want to live," and no, I couldn't go shopping without fear in our low-income neighborhoods.

The idea that any ol' white person can find a publisher for a piece is most certainly a symptom of class privilege. Having come from a family of people who didn't even graduate from high school, who knew not a single academic or intellectual person, it would never occur to me to assume that I could be published. It is absolutely a freak anomaly that I'm in graduate school, considering that not one person on either side of my family has a college degree. And it took me until my 30s to ever believe that someone from my stock could achieve such a thing. Poverty colors nearly everything about your perspective on opportunities for advancement in life. Middle-class, educated people assume that anyone can achieve their goals if they work hard enough. Folks steeped in poverty rarely see a life past working at the gas station, making the rent on their trailer, and self-medicating with cigarettes and prescription drugs until they die of a heart attack. (I've just described one whole side of my family and the life I assumed I'd be living before I lucked out of it.)

I, maybe more than most people, can completely understand why broke white folks get pissed when the word "privilege" is thrown around. As a child I was constantly discriminated against because of my poverty, and those wounds still run very deep. But luckily my college education introduced me to a more nuanced concept of privilege: the term "intersectionality." The concept of intersectionality recognizes that people can be privileged in some ways and definitely not privileged in others. There are many different types of privilege, not just skin-color privilege, that impact the way people can move through the world or are discriminated against. These are all things you are born into, not things you earned, that afford you opportunities that others may not have. For example:

- **Citizenship:** Simply being born in this country affords you certain privileges that non-citizens will never access.

- **Class:** Being born into a financially stable family can help guarantee your health, happiness, safety, education, intelligence, and future opportunities.
- **Sexual orientation:** If you were born straight, every state in this country affords you privileges that non-straight folks have to fight the Supreme Court for.
- **Sex:** If you were born male, you can assume that you can walk through a parking garage without worrying that you'll be raped and then have to deal with a defense attorney blaming it on what you were wearing.
- **Ability:** If you were born able-bodied, you probably don't have to plan your life around handicap access, braille, or other special needs.
- **Gender identity:** If you were born cisgender (that is, your gender identity matches the sex you were assigned at birth), you don't have to worry that using the restroom or locker room will invoke public outrage.

As you can see, belonging to one or more category of privilege, especially being a straight, white, middle-class, able-bodied male, can be like winning a lottery you didn't even know you were playing. But this is not to imply that any form of privilege is exactly the same as another, or that people lacking in one area of privilege understand what it's like to be lacking in other areas. Race discrimination is not equal to sex discrimination and so forth.

And listen: Recognizing privilege doesn't mean suffering guilt or shame for your lot in life. Nobody's saying that straight, white, middle-class, able-bodied males are all a bunch of assholes who don't work hard for what they have. Recognizing privilege simply means being aware that some people have to work much harder just to experience the things you take for granted (if they ever can experience them at all).

I know now that I *am* privileged in many ways. I am privileged as a natural-born white citizen. I am privileged as a cisgender woman. I am privileged as an able-bodied person. I am privileged that my first language is also our national language, and that I was born with an intellect and ambition that pulled me out of the poverty that I was otherwise destined for. I was privileged to be able to marry my way "up" by partnering with a privileged, middle-class, educated male who fully expected me to earn a college degree.

There are a million ways I experience privilege, and some that I certainly don't. But thankfully, intersectionality allows us to examine these varying dimensions and degrees of discrimination while raising awareness of the results of multiple systems of oppression at work.

Tell me: Are you a white person who's felt uncomfortable with the term "white privilege"? Does a more nuanced approach help you see your own privilege more clearly?

PART 3

Writing With Research

Annoying Ways People Use Sources

Kyle D. Stedman

HOW SLOW DRIVING IS LIKE SLOPPY WRITING

I hate slow drivers. When I'm driving in the fast lane, maintaining the speed limit exactly, and I find myself behind someone who thinks the fast lane is for people who drive ten miles per hour *below* the speed limit, I get an annoyed feeling in my chest like hot water filling a heavy bucket. I wave my arms around and yell, "What . . . ? But, hey . . . oh come *on!*" There are at least two explanations for why some slow drivers fail to move out of the way:

1. They don't know that the generally accepted practice of highway driving in the U.S. is to move to the right if an upcoming car wants to pass. Or,
2. They know the guidelines but don't care.

But here's the thing: writers can forget that their readers are sometimes just as annoyed at writing that fails to follow conventions as drivers are when stuck behind a car that fails to move over. In other words, there's something similar between these two people: the knowledgeable driver who thinks, "I thought all drivers *knew* that the left lane is for the fastest cars," and the reader who thinks, "I thought all writers *knew* that outside sources should be introduced, punctuated, and cited according to a set of standards."

One day, you may discover that something you've written has just been read by a reader who, unfortunately, was annoyed at some of the ways you integrated sources. She was reading along and then suddenly exclaimed, "What . . . ? But, hey . . . oh come *on!*" If you're lucky, this reader will try to imagine why you typed things the way you did, giving you the benefit of the doubt. But sometimes you'll be slotted into positions that might not really be accurate. When this frustrated reader walks away from your work, trying to figure out, say, why you used so many quotations, or why you kept starting and ending paragraphs with them, she may come to the same conclusions I do about slow drivers:

1. You don't know the generally accepted practices of using sources (especially in academic writing) in the U.S. Or,
2. You know the guidelines but don't care.

And it will be a lot harder for readers to take you seriously if they think you're ignorant or rude.

This judgment, of course, will often be unfair. These readers might completely ignore the merits of your insightful, stylistically beautiful, or revolutionarily important language—just as my anger at another driver makes me fail to admire his custom paint job. But readers and writers don't always see eye to eye on the same text. In fact, some things I write about in this essay will only bother your pickiest readers (some teachers, some editors, some snobby friends), while many other readers might zoom past how you use sources without blinking. But in my experience, I find that teachers do a disservice when we fail to alert students to the kind of things that some readers might be annoyed at—however illogical these things sometimes seem. People are often unreasonably picky, and writers have to deal with that—which they do by trying to anticipate and preemptively fix whatever might annoy a broad range of readers. Plus, the more effectively you anticipate that pickiness, the more likely it is that readers will interpret your quotations and paraphrases in the way you want them to—critically or acceptingly, depending on your writing context.

It helps me to remember that the conventions of writing have a fundamentally *rhetorical* nature. That is, I follow different conventions depending on the purpose and audience of my writing, because I know that I'll come across differently to different people depending on how well I follow the conventions expected in any particular writing space. In a blog, I cite a source by hyperlinking; in an academic essay, I use a parenthetical citation that refers to a list of references at the end of the essay. One of the fundamental ideas of rhetoric is that speakers/writers/composers shape what they say/write/create based on what they want it to do, where they're publishing it, and what they know about their audience/readers. And those decisions include nitty-gritty things like introducing quotations and citing paraphrases clearly: not everyone in the entire world approaches these things the same way, but when I strategically learn the expectations of my U.S. academic audience, what I really want to say comes across smoothly, without little annoying blips in my readers' experience. Notice that I'm not saying that there's a particular *right* or *wrong* way to use conventions in my writing—if the modern U.S. academic system had evolved from a primarily African or Asian or Latin American cultural consciousness instead of a European one, conventions for writing would probably be very different. That's why they're *conventions* and not *rules.*

THE ANNOYANCES

Because I'm not here to tell you *rules, decrees,* or *laws,* it makes sense to call my classifications *annoyances.* In the examples that follow, I wrote all of the annoying examples myself, but all the examples I use of good writing come from actual student papers in first year composition classes at my university; I have their permission to quote them.

Armadillo Roadkill

> *Armadillo Roadkill:* dropping in a quotation without introducing it first

Everyone in the car hears it: buh-BUMP. The driver insists to the passengers, "But that armadillo—I didn't see it! It just came out of nowhere!"

Sadly, a poorly introduced quotation can lead readers to a similar exclamation: "It just came out of nowhere!" And though readers probably won't experience the same level of grief and regret when surprised by a quotation as opposed to an armadillo, I submit that there's a kinship between the experiences: both involve a normal, pleasant activity (driving; reading) stopped suddenly short by an unexpected barrier (a sudden armadillo; a sudden quotation).

Here's an example of what I'm talking about:

> We should all be prepared with a backup plan if a zombie invasion occurs. "Unlike its human counterparts, an army of zombies is completely independent of support" (Brooks 155). Preparations should be made in the following areas. . . .

Did you notice how the quotation is dropped in without any kind of warning? (Buh-BUMP.)

The Fix: The easiest way to effectively massage in quotations is by purposefully returning to each one in your draft to see if you set the stage for your readers—often, by signaling that a quote is about to come, stating who the quote came from, and showing how your readers should interpret it. In the above example, that could be done by introducing the quotation with something like this (new text bolded):

> We should all be prepared with a backup plan if a zombie invasion occurs. **Max Brooks suggests a number of ways to prepare for zombies' particular traits, though he underestimates the ability of humans to survive in harsh environments. For example, he writes,** "Unlike its human counterparts, an army of zombies is completely independent of support" (155). **His shortsightedness could have a number of consequences. . . .**

In this version, I know a quotation is coming ("For example"), I know it's going to be written by Max Brooks, and I know I'm being asked to read the quote rather skeptically ("he underestimates"). The sentence with the quotation itself also now begins with a "tag" that eases us into it ("he writes").

Here's an actual example from Alexsandra. Notice the way she builds up to the quotation and then explains it:

> In the first two paragraphs, the author takes a defensive position when explaining the perception that the public has about scientists by saying that "there is anxiety that scientists lack both wisdom and social responsibility and are so motivated by ambition" and "scientists are repeatedly referred to as 'playing God'" (Wolpert 345). With this last sentence especially, his tone seems to demonstrate how he uses the ethos appeal to initially set a tone of someone that is tired of being misunderstood.

Alexsandra prepares us for the quotation, quotes, and then analyzes it. I love it. This isn't a hard and fast rule—I've seen it broken by the best of writers, I admit—but it's a wise standard to hold yourself to unless you have a reason not to.

Dating Spider-Man

> *Dating Spider-Man:* starting or ending a paragraph with a quotation

An annoyance that's closely connected to Armadillo Roadkill is the tendency writers sometimes have of starting or ending paragraphs with quotations. This isn't technically *wrong*, and there are situations when the effect of surprise is what you're going for. But often, a paragraph-beginning or paragraph-closing quotation feels rushed, unexplained, disjointed.

It's like dating Spider-Man. You're walking along with him and he says something remarkably interesting—but then he tilts his head, hearing something far away, and suddenly shoots a web onto the nearest building and *zooms* away through the air. As if you had just read an interesting quotation dangling at the end of a paragraph, you wanted to hear more of his opinion, but it's too late—he's already moved on. Later, he suddenly jumps off a balcony and is by your side again, and he starts talking about something you don't understand. You're confused because he just dropped in and expected you to understand the context of what was on his mind at that moment, much like when readers step into a paragraph that begins with a quotation. Here's an example:

> *[End of a preceding paragraph:]* . . . Therefore, the evidence clearly suggests that we should be exceptionally careful about deciding when and where to rest.

> "When taking a nap, always rest your elbow on your desk and keep your arm perpendicular to your desktop" (Piven and Borgenicht 98). After all, consider the following scenario. . . .

There's a perfectly good reason why this feels odd—which should feel familiar after reading about the Armadillo Roadkill annoyance above. When you got to the quotation in the second paragraph, you didn't know what you were supposed to think about it; there was no guidance.

The Fix is the same: in the majority of situations, readers appreciate being guided to and led away from a quotation by the writer doing the quoting. Readers get a sense of pleasure from the safe flow of hearing how to read an upcoming quotation, reading it, and then being told one way to interpret it. Prepare, quote, analyze.

I mentioned above that there can be situations where starting a paragraph with a quotation can have a strong effect. Personally, I usually enjoy this most at the beginning of essays or the beginning of sections—like in this example from the very beginning of Jennifer's essay:

> "Nothing is ever simple: Racism and nobility can exist in the same man, hate and love in the same woman, fear and loyalty, compromise and idealism, all the yin-yang dichotomies that make the human species so utterly confounding, yet so utterly fascinating" (Hunter). The hypocrisy and complexity that Stephen Hunter from the *Washington Post* describes is the basis of the movie *Crash* (2004).

Instantly, her quotation hooks me. It doesn't feel thoughtless, like it would feel if I continued to be whisked to quotations without preparation throughout the essay. But please don't overdo it; any quotation that opens an essay or section ought to be integrally related to your topic (as is Jennifer's), not just a cheap gimmick.

Uncle Barry and His Encyclopedia of Useless Information

Uncle Barry and His Encyclopedia of Useless Information: using too many quotations in a row

You probably know someone like this: a person (for me, my Uncle Barry) who constantly tries to impress me with how much he knows about just about everything. I might casually bring up something in the news ("Wow, these health care debates are getting really heated, aren't they?") and then find myself barraged by all of Uncle Barry's ideas on government-sponsored health care—which *then* drifts into a story about how his cousin Maxine died in an underfunded hospice center, which had a parking lot that he could have designed better, which reminds him of how good he is at fixing things, just like the garage door at my parents' house, which probably only needs a little . . . You get the idea. I might even think to myself, "Wait, I want to know more about that topic, but you're zooming on before you contextualize your information at all."

This is something like reading an essay that relies too much on quotations. Readers get the feeling that they're moving from one quotation to the next without ever quite getting to hear the *real* point of what the author wants to say, never getting any time to form an opinion about the claims. In fact, this often makes it sound as if the author has almost no authority at all. You may have been annoyed by paragraphs like this before:

> Addressing this issue, David M. Potter comments, "Whether Seward meant this literally or not, it was in fact a singularly accurate forecast for territorial Kansas" (199). Of course, Potter's view is contested, even though he claims, "Soon, the Missourians began to perceive the advantages of operating without publicity" (200). Interestingly, "The election was bound to be irregular in any case" (201).

Wait—huh? This author feels like Uncle Barry to me: grabbing right and left for topics (or quotes) in an effort to sound authoritative.

The Fix is to return to each quotation and decide why it's there and then massage it in accordingly. If you just want to use a quote to cite a *fact,* then consider paraphrasing or summarizing the source material (which I find is usually harder than it sounds but is usually worth it for the smoothness my paragraph gains). But if you quoted because you want to draw attention to the source's particular phrasing, or if you want to respond to something you agree with or disagree with in the source, then consider taking the time to surround *each* quotation with guidance to your readers about what you want them to think about that quote.

In the following passage, I think Jessica demonstrates a balance between source and analysis well. Notice that she only uses a single quotation, even though she surely could have chosen more. But instead, Jessica relies on her instincts and remains the primary voice of authority in the passage:

> Robin Toner's article, "Feminist Pitch by a Democrat named Obama," was written a week after the video became public and is partially a response to it. She writes, "The Obama campaign is, in some ways, subtly marketing its candidate as a post-feminist man, a generation beyond the gender conflicts of the boomers." Subtly is the key word. Obama is a passive character throughout the video, never directly addressing the camera. Rather, he is shown indirectly through speeches, intimate conversations with supporters and candid interaction with family. This creates a sense of intimacy, which in turn creates a feeling of trust.

Toner's response to the Obama video is like a diving board that Jessica bounces off of before she gets to the really interesting stuff: the pool (her own observations). A bunch of diving boards lined up without a pool (tons of quotes with no analysis) wouldn't please anyone—except maybe Uncle Barry.

Am I in the Right Movie?

Am I in the Right Movie? Failing to integrate a quotation into the grammar of the preceding sentence

When reading drafts of my writing, this is a common experience: I start to read a sentence that seems interesting and normal, with everything going just the way I expect it to. But then the unexpected happens: a quotation blurts itself into the sentence in a way that doesn't fit with the grammar that built up to quotation. It feels like sitting in a movie theater, everything going as expected, when suddenly the opening credits start for a movie I didn't plan to see. Here are two examples of what I'm talking about. Read them out loud, and you'll see how suddenly wrong they feel.

1. Therefore, the author warns that a zombie's vision "are no different than those of a normal human" (Brooks 6).
2. Sheila Anne Barry advises that "Have you ever wondered what it's like to walk on a tightrope—many feet up in the air?" (50)

In the first example, the quoter's build-up to the quotation uses a singular subject—*a zombie's vision*—which, when paired with the quotation, is annoyingly matched with the plural verb *are.* It would be much less jolting to write, "a zombie's vision *is,*" which makes the subject and verb agree. In the second example, the quoter builds up to the quotation with a third-person, declarative independent clause: *Sheila Anne Barry advises.* But then the quotation switches into second person—*you*—and unexpectedly asks a question—completely different from the expectation that was built up by the first part of the sentence.

The Fix is usually easy: you read your essay out loud to someone else, and if you stumble as you enter a quotation, there's probably something you can adjust in your lead-in sentence to make the two fit together well. Maybe you'll need to choose a different subject to make it fit with the quote's verb (*reader* instead of *readers; each* instead of *all*), or maybe you'll have to scrap what you first wrote and start over. On occasion you'll even feel the need to transparently modify the quotation by adding an [s] to one of its verbs, always being certain to use square brackets to show that you adjusted something in the quotation. Maybe you'll even find a way to quote a shorter part of the quotation and squeeze it into the context of a sentence that is mostly your own, a trick that can have a positive effect on readers, who like smooth water slides more than they like bumpy slip-and-slides. Jennifer does this well in the following sentence, for example:

> In *Crash,* no character was allowed to "escape his own hypocrisy" (Muller), and the film itself emphasized that the reason there is so much racial tension among strangers is because of the personal issues one cannot deal with alone.

She saw a phrase that she liked in Muller's article, so she found a way to work it in smoothly, without the need for a major break in her thought. Let's put ourselves in Jennifer's shoes for a moment: it's possible that she started drafting this sentence using the plural subject *characters,* writing "In *Crash,* no characters were allowed . . ." But then, imagine she looked back at the quote from Muller and saw that it said "escape *his* own hypocrisy," which was a clue that she had to change the first part of her sentence to match the singular construction of the quote.

I Can't Find the Stupid Link

I Can't Find the Stupid Link: no connection between the first letter of a parenthetical citation and the first letter of a works cited entry

You've been in this situation: you're on a website that seems like it might be interesting and you want to learn more about it. But the home page doesn't tell you much, so you look for an "About Us" or "More Information" or "FAQ" link. But no matter where you search—Top of page? Bottom? Left menu?—you can't find the stupid link. This is usually the fault of web designers, who don't always take the time to test their sites as much as they should with actual users. The communication failure here is simple: you're used to finding certain kinds of basic information in the places people usually put it. If it's not there, you're annoyed.

Similarly, a reader might see a citation and have a quick internal question about it: *What journal was this published in? When was it published? Is this an article I could find online to skim myself? This author has a sexy last name—I wonder what his first name is?* Just like when you look for a link to more information, this reader has a simple, quick question that he or she expects to answer easily. And the most basic way for readers to answer those questions (when they're reading a work written in APA or MLA style) is (1) to look at the information in the citation, and (2) skim the references or works cited section alphabetically, looking for the first letter in the citation. There's an assumption that the first letter of a citation will be the letter to look for in the list of works cited.

In short, the following may annoy readers who want to quickly learn more about the citation:

> *[Essay Text:]* A respected guide on the subject suggests, "If possible, always take the high ground and hold it" (*The Zombie Survival Guide* 135).
>
> *[Works Cited Page:]* Brooks, Max. *The Zombie Survival Guide: Complete Protection from the Living Dead.* New York: Three Rivers, 2003. Print.

The reader may wonder when *The Zombie Survival Guide* was published and flip back to the works cited page, but the parenthetical citation sends her straight to the *Z*'s in the works cited list (because initial *A*'s and *The*'s are ignored when alphabetizing). However, the complete works cited entry is actually with the *B*'s (where it belongs).

The Fix is to make sure that the first word of the works cited entry is the word you use in your in-text citation, every time. If the works cited entry starts with Brooks, use (Brooks) in the essay text.

Citations not including last names may seem to complicate this advice, but they all follow the same basic concept. For instance, you might have:

- **A citation that only lists a title.** For instance, your citation might read ("Gray Wolf General Information"). In this case, the assumption is that the citation can be found under the *G* section of the works cited page. Leah cites her paraphrase of a source with no author in the following way, indicating that I should head to the *G*'s if I want to learn more about her source:

  > Alaska is the only refuge that is left for the wolves in the United States, and once that is gone, they will more than likely become extinct in this country ("Gray Wolf General Information").

- **A citation that only lists a page number.** Maybe the citation simply says (25). That implies that somewhere in the surrounding text, the essay writer must have made it stupendously clear what name or title to look up in the works cited list. This happens a lot, since it's common to introduce a quotation by naming the person it came from, in which case it would be repetitive to name that author again in the citation.
- **A quotation without a citation at all.** This happens when you cite a work that is both (A) from a web page that doesn't number the pages or paragraphs and (B) is named in the text surrounding the quotation. Readers will assume that the author is named nearby. Stephanie wisely leaves off any citation in the example below, where it's already clear that I should head to the *O*'s on the works cited page to find information about this source, a web page written by Opotow:

> To further this point, Opotow notes, "Don't imagine you'll be unscathed by the methods you use. The end may justify the means . . . But there's a price to pay, and the price does tend to be oneself."

I Swear I Did Some Research!

Let's look in depth at this potentially annoying passage from a hypothetical student paper:

> *I Swear I Did Some Research:* dropping in a citation without making it clear what information came from that source

> It's possible that a multidisciplinary approach to understanding the universe will open new doors of understanding. If theories from sociology, communication, and philosophy joined with physics, the possibilities would be boundless. This would inspire new research, much like in the 1970s when scientists changed their focus from grand-scale theories of the universe to the small concerns of quantum physics (Hawking 51).

In at least two ways, this is stellar material. First, the author is actually voicing a point of view; she sounds knowledgeable, strong. Second, and more to the point of this chapter, the author includes a citation, showing that she knows that ethical citation standards ask authors to cite paraphrases and summaries—not just quotations.

But on the other hand, which of these three sentences, exactly, came from Hawking's book? Did *Hawking* claim that physics experts should join up with folks in other academic disciplines, or is that the student writer? In other words, at which point does the author's point of view meld into material taken specifically from Hawking?

I recognize that there often aren't clean answers to a question like that. What we read and what we know sometimes meld together so unnoticeably that we don't know which ideas and pieces of information are "ours" and which aren't. Discussing "patchwriting," a term used to describe writing that blends words and phrases from sources with words and phrases we came up with ourselves, scholar Rebecca Moore Howard writes, "When I believe I am not patchwriting, I am simply doing it so expertly that the seams are no longer visible—or I am doing it so unwittingly that I cannot cite my sources" (91). In other words, *all* the moves we make when writing came from somewhere else at some point, whether we realize it or not. Yikes. But remember our main purpose here: to not look annoying when using sources. And most of your instructors aren't going to say, "I understand that I couldn't tell the difference between your ideas and your source's because we quite naturally patchwrite all the time. That's fine with me. Party on!" They're much more likely to imagine that you plopped in a few extra citations as a way of defensively saying, "I swear I did some research! See? Here's a citation right here! Doesn't that prove I worked really hard?"

The Fix: Write the sentences preceding the citation with *specific words and phrases that will tell readers what information came from where.* Like this (bolded words are new):

> It's possible that a multidisciplinary approach to understanding the universe will open new doors of understanding. **I believe that** if theories from sociology, communication, and philosophy joined with physics, the possibilities would be boundless. This would inspire new research, much like **the changes Stephen Hawking describes happening** in the 1970s when scientists changed their focus from grand-scale theories of the universe to the small concerns of quantum physics (51).

Perhaps these additions could still use some stylistic editing for wordiness and flow, but the source-related job is done: readers know exactly which claims the essay writer is making and which ones Hawking made in his book. The last sentence and only the last sentence summarizes the ideas Hawking describes on page 51 of his book.

One warning: you'll find that scholars in some disciplines (especially in the sciences and social sciences) use citations in the way I just warned you to avoid. You might see sentences like this one, from page 64 of Glenn Gordon Smith, Ana T. Torres-Ayala, and Allen J. Heindel's article in the *Journal of Distance Education:*

> Some researchers have suggested "curriculum" as a key element in the design of web-based courses (Berge, 1998; Driscoll, 1998; Meyen, Tangen, & Lian, 1999; Wiens & Gunter, 1998).

Whoa—that's a lot of citations. Remember how the writer of my earlier example cited Stephen Hawking because she summarized his ideas? Well, a number of essays describing the results of experiments, like this one, use citations with a different purpose, citing previous studies whose general conclusions support the study described in this new paper, like building blocks. It's like saying to your potentially skeptical readers, "Look, you might be wondering if I'm a quack. But I can prove I'm not! See, all these other people published in similar areas! Are you going to pick fights with all of *them* too?" You might have noticed as well that these citations are in APA format, reflecting the standards of the social sciences journal this passage was published in. Well, in this kind of context APA's requirement to cite the year of a study makes a lot of sense too—after all, the older a study, the less likely it is to still be relevant.

CONCLUSION: USE YOUR TURN SIGNALS

You may have guessed the biggest weakness in an essay like this: what's annoying varies from person to person, with some readers happily skimming past awkward introductions to quotations without a blink, while others see a paragraph-opening quotation as something to complain about on Facebook. All I've given you here—all I *can* give you unless I actually get to know you and your various writing contexts—are the basics that will apply in a number of academic writing contexts. Think of these as signals to your readers about your intentions, much as wise drivers rely on their turn signals to communicate their intentions to other drivers. In some cases when driving, signaling is an almost artistic decision, relying on the gut reaction of the driver to interpret what is best in times when the law doesn't mandate use one way or the other. I hope your writing is full of similar signals. Now if I could only convince the guy driving in front of me to use *his* blinker. . . .

Works Cited

Barry, Sheila Anne. *Tricks & Pranks to Fool Your Friends.* New York: Sterling, 1984. Print.

Brooks, Max. *The Zombie Survival Guide: Complete Protection from the Living Dead.* New York: Three Rivers, 2003. Print.

"Gray Wolf General Information." *Environmental Conservation Online System.* U.S. Fish and Wildlife Service, 15 Oct. 2008. Web. 23 Oct. 2008.

Hawking, Stephen. *A Brief History of Time: From the Big Bang to Black Holes.* New York: Bantam, 1988. Print.

Howard, Rebecca Moore. "The New Abolitionism Comes to Plagiarism." *Perspectives on Plagiarism and Intellectual Property in a Postmodern World.* Ed. Lisa Buranen and Alice M. Roy. Albany: SUNY P, 1999. 87–95. Print.

Hunter, Stephen. "'Crash': The Collision Of Human Contradictions." *The Washington Post.* The Washington Post Company, 6 May 2005. Web. 21 Feb. 2008.

Muller, Bill. "Crash: LA Tale Confronts, Then Shatters, Stereotypes." *The Arizona Republic.* AZCentral.com, 6 May 2005. Web. 21 Feb. 2008.

Opotow, Susan. "Moral Exclusion and Torture: The Ticking Bomb Scenario and the Slippery Ethical Slope." *Peace and Conflict Studies* 13.4 (2007): 457–61. *PsycINFO.* Web. 27 Sept. 2008.

Piven, Joshua, and David Borgenicht. *The Worst-Case Scenario Survival Handbook: Work.* San Francisco: Chronicle, 2003. Print.

Potter, David M. *The Impending Crisis: 1848–1861.* Ed. Don E. Fehrenbacher. New York: Harper & Row, 1976. Print.

Smith, Glenn Gordon, Ana T. Torres-Ayala, and Allen J. Heindel. "Disciplinary Differences in E-learning Instructional Design: The Case of Mathematics." *Journal of Distance Education* 22.3 (2008): 63–88. Web. 10 Sept. 2009.

Toner, Robin. "Feminist Pitch by a Democrat Named Obama." *The New York Times.* The New York Times Company, 2 Dec. 2007. Web. 22 Oct. 2008.

Wolpert, Lewis. "Is Cell Science Dangerous?" *Journal of Medical Ethics* 33.6 (2007): 345–48. *Academic Search Premier.* Web. 28 Jan. 2009.

Introduction to Primary Research: Observations, Surveys, and Interviews

Dana Lynn Driscoll

PRIMARY RESEARCH: DEFINITIONS AND OVERVIEW

How research is defined varies widely from field to field, and as you progress through your college career, your coursework will teach you much more about what it means to be a researcher within your field. For example, engineers, who focus on applying scientific knowledge to develop designs, processes, and objects, conduct research using simulations, mathematical models, and a variety of tests to see how well their designs work. Sociologists conduct research using surveys, interviews, observations, and statistical analysis to better understand people, societies, and cultures. Graphic designers conduct research through locating images for reference for their artwork and engaging in background research on clients and companies to best serve their needs. Historians conduct research by examining archival materials—newspapers, journals, letters, and other surviving texts—and through conducting oral history interviews. Research is not limited to what has already been written or found at the library, also known as secondary research. Rather, individuals conducting research are *producing* the articles and reports found in a library database or in a book. Primary research, the focus of this essay, is research that is collected firsthand rather than found in a book, database, or journal.

Primary research is often based on principles of the scientific method, a theory of investigation first developed by John Stuart Mill in the nineteenth century in his book *Philosophy of the Scientific Method.* Although the application of the scientific method varies from field to field, the general principles of the scientific method allow researchers to learn more about the world and observable phenomena. Using the scientific method, researchers develop research questions or hypotheses and collect data on events, objects, or people that is measurable, observable, and replicable. The ultimate goal in conducting primary research is to learn about something new that can be confirmed by others and to eliminate our own biases in the process.

Essay Overview and Student Examples

The essay begins by providing an overview of ethical considerations when conducting primary research, and then covers the stages that you will go through in your primary research: planning, collecting, analyzing, and writing. After the four stages comes an introduction to three common ways of conducting primary research in first year writing classes:

- *Observations.* Observing and measuring the world around you, including observations of people and other measurable events.
- *Interviews.* Asking participants questions in a one-on-one or small group setting.
- *Surveys.* Asking participants about their opinions and behaviors through a short questionnaire.

In addition, we will be examining two student projects that used substantial portions of primary research:

Derek Laan, a nutrition major at Purdue University, wanted to learn more about student eating habits on campus. His primary research included observations of the campus food courts, student behavior while in the food courts, and a survey of students' daily food intake. His secondary research included looking at national student eating trends on college campuses, information from the United States Food and Drug Administration, and books on healthy eating.

Jared Schwab, an agricultural and biological engineering major at Purdue, was interested in learning more about how writing and communication took place in his field. His primary research included interviewing a professional engineer and a student who was a senior majoring in engineering. His secondary research included examining journals, books, professional organizations, and writing guides within the field of engineering.

ETHICS OF PRIMARY RESEARCH

Both projects listed above included primary research on human participants; therefore, Derek and Jared both had to consider research ethics throughout their primary research process. As Earl Babbie writes in *The Practice of Social Research,* throughout the early and middle parts of the twentieth century researchers took advantage of participants and treated them unethically. During World War II, Nazi doctors performed heinous experiments on prisoners without their consent, while in the U.S., a number of medical and psychological experiments caused patients undue mental and physical trauma and, in some cases, death. Because of these and other similar events, many nations have established ethical laws and guidelines for researchers who work with human participants. In the United States, the guidelines for the ethical treatment of human research participants are described in *The Belmont Report,* released in 1979. Today, universities have Institutional Review Boards (or IRBs) that oversee research. Students conducting research as part of a class may not need permission from the university's IRB, although they still need to ensure that they follow ethical guidelines in research. The following provides a brief overview of ethical considerations:

- *Voluntary participation. The Belmont Report* suggests that, in most cases, you need to get permission from people before you involve them in any primary research you are conducting. If you are doing a survey or interview, your participants must first agree to fill out your survey or to be interviewed. Consent for observations can be more complicated, and is discussed later in the essay.
- *Confidentiality and anonymity.* Your participants may reveal embarrassing or potentially damaging information such as racist

comments or unconventional behavior. In these cases, you should keep your participants' identities anonymous when writing your results. An easy way to do this is to create a "pseudonym" (or false name) for them so that their identity is protected.

- *Researcher bias.* There is little point in collecting data and learning about something if you already think you know the answer! Bias might be present in the way you ask questions, the way you take notes, or the conclusions you draw from the data you collect.

The above are only three of many considerations when involving human participants in your primary research. For a complete understanding of ethical considerations please refer to *The Belmont Report.*

Now that we have considered the ethical implications of research, we will examine how to formulate research questions and plan your primary research project.

PLANNING YOUR PRIMARY RESEARCH PROJECT

The primary research process is quite similar to the writing process, and you can draw upon your knowledge of the writing process to understand the steps involved in a primary research project. Just like in the writing process, a successful primary research project begins with careful planning and background research. This section first describes how to create a research timeline to help plan your research. It then walks you through the planning stages by examining when primary research is useful or appropriate for your first year composition course, narrowing down a topic, and developing research questions.

The Research Timeline

When you begin to conduct any kind of primary research, creating a timeline will help keep you on task. Because students conducting primary research usually focus on the collection of data itself, they often overlook the equally important areas of planning (invention), analyzing data, and writing. To help manage your time, you should create a research timeline, such as the sample timeline presented here.

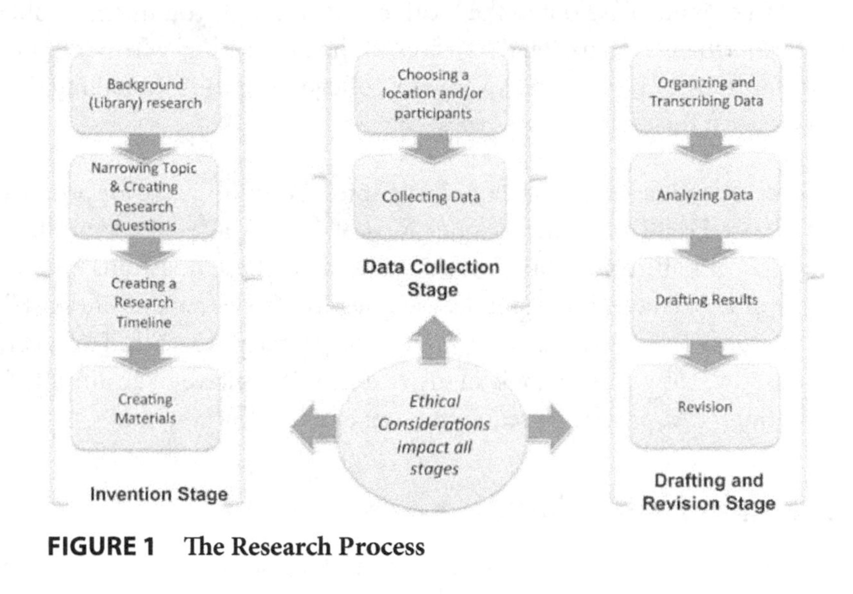

FIGURE 1 The Research Process

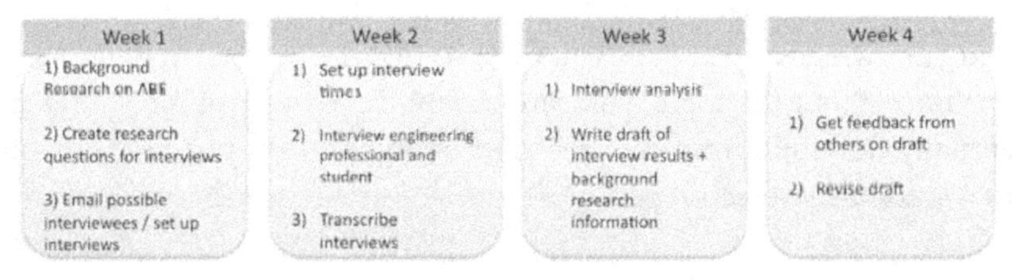

FIGURE 2 A Sample Timeline for Jared's Research Project

When Primary Research Is Useful or Appropriate

In *Evaluating Scientific Research: Separating Fact from Fiction*, Fred Leavitt explains that primary research is useful for questions that can be answered through asking others and direct observation. For first year writing courses, primary research is particularly useful when you want to learn about a problem that does not have a wealth of published information. This may be because the problem is a recent event or it is something not commonly studied. For example, if you are writing a paper on a new political issue, such as changes in tax laws or healthcare, you might not be able to find a wealth of peer-reviewed research because the issue is only several weeks old. You may find it necessary to collect some of your own data on the issue to supplement what you found at the library. Primary research is also useful when you are studying a local problem or learning how a larger issue plays out at the local level. Although you might be able to find information on national statistics for healthy eating, whether or not those statistics are representative of your college campus is something that you can learn through primary research.

However, not all research questions and topics are appropriate for primary research. As Fred Leavitt writes, questions of an ethical, philosophical, or metaphysical nature are not appropriate because these questions are not testable or observable. For example, the question "Does an afterlife exist?" is not a question that can be answered with primary research. However, the question "How many people in my community believe in an afterlife?" is something that primary research can answer.

Narrowing Your Topic

Just like the writing process, you should start your primary research process with secondary (library) research to learn more about what is already known and what gaps you need to fill with your own data. As you learn more about the topic, you can narrow down your interest area and eventually develop a research question or hypothesis, just as you would with a secondary research paper.

Developing Research Questions or Hypotheses

As John Stuart Mill describes, primary research can use both *inductive* and *deductive* approaches, and the type approach is usually based on the field of inquiry. Some fields use *deductive reasoning,* where researchers start with a hypothesis or general conclusion and then collect specific data to support or refute their hypothesis. Other fields use *inductive reasoning,* where researchers start with a question and collect information that eventually leads to a conclusion.

Once you have spent some time reviewing the secondary research on your topic, you are ready to write a primary research question or hypothesis. A research question or hypothesis should be something that is specific, narrow, and discoverable through primary research methods. Just like a thesis statement for a paper, if your research question or hypothesis is too broad, your research will be unfocused and your data will be difficult to analyze and write about. Here is a set of sample research questions:

> *Poor Research Question:* What do college students think of politics and the economy?
>
> *Revised Research Question:* What do students at Purdue University believe about the current economic crisis in terms of economic recoverability?

The poor research question is unspecific as to what group of students the researcher is interested in—i.e. students in the U.S.? In a particular state? At their university? The poor research question was also too broad; terms like "politics" and the "economy" cover too much ground for a single project. The revised question narrows down the topic to students at a particular university and focuses on a specific issue related to the economy: economic recoverability. The research question could also be rephrased as a testable hypothesis using deductive reasoning: "Purdue University college students are well informed about economic recoverability plans." Because they were approaching their projects in an exploratory, inductive manner, both Derek and Jared chose to ask research questions:

> Derek: Are students' eating habits at Purdue University healthy or unhealthy? What are the causes of students' eating behavior?
>
> Jared: What are the major features of writing and communication in agricultural and biological engineering? What are the major controversies?

A final step in working with a research question or hypothesis is determining what key terms you are using and how you will define them. Before conducting his research, Derek had to define the terms "healthy" and "unhealthy"; for this, he used the USDA's Food Pyramid as a guide. Similarly, part of what Jared focused on in his interviews was learning more about how agricultural and biological engineers defined terms like "writing" and "communication." Derek and Jared thought carefully about the terms within their research questions and how these terms might be measured.

Choosing a Data Collection Method

Once you have formulated a research question or hypothesis, you will need to make decisions about what kind of data you can collect that will best address your research topic. Derek chose to examine eating habits by observing both what students ate at lunch and surveying students about eating behavior. Jared decided that in-depth interviews with experienced individuals in his field would provide him with the best information.

To choose a data collection method for your research question, read through the next sections on observations, interviews, and surveys.

OBSERVATIONS

Observations have led to some of the most important scientific discoveries in human history. Charles Darwin used observations of the animal and marine life at the Galapagos Islands to help him formulate his theory of evolution that he describes in *On the Origin of Species.* Today, social scientists, natural scientists, engineers, computer scientists, educational researchers, and many others use observations as a primary research method.

Observations can be conducted on nearly any subject matter, and the kinds of observations you will do depend on your research question. You might observe traffic or parking patterns on campus to get a sense of what improvements could be made. You might observe clouds, plants, or other natural phenomena. If you choose to observe people, you will have several additional considerations including the manner in which you will observe them and gain their consent.

If you are observing people, you can choose between two common ways to observe: participant observation and unobtrusive observation. Participant observation is a common method within ethnographic research in sociology and anthropology. In this kind of observation, a researcher may interact with participants and become part of their community. Margaret Mead, a famous anthropologist, spent extended periods of time living in, and interacting with, communities that she studied. Conversely, in unobtrusive observation, you do not interact with participants but rather simply record their behavior. Although in most circumstances people must volunteer to be participants in research, in some cases it is acceptable to not let participants know you are observing them. In places that people perceive as public, such as a campus food court or a shopping mall, people do not expect privacy, and so it is generally acceptable to observe without participant consent. In places that people perceive as private, which can include a church, home, classroom, or even an intimate conversation at a restaurant, participant consent should be sought.

The second issue about participant consent in terms of unobtrusive observation is whether or not getting consent is feasible for the study. If you are observing people in a busy airport, bus station, or campus food court, getting participant consent may be next to impossible. In Derek's study of student eating habits on campus, he went to the campus food courts during meal times and observed students purchasing food. Obtaining participant consent for his observations would have been next to impossible because hundreds of students were coming through the food court during meal times. Since Derek's research was in a place that participants would perceive as public, it was not practical to get their consent, and since his data was anonymous, he did not violate their privacy.

Eliminating Bias in Your Observation Notes

The ethical concern of being unbiased is important in recording your observations. You need to be aware of the difference between an observation (recording exactly what you see) and an interpretation (making assumptions and judgments about what you see). When you observe, you should focus first on only the events that are directly observable. Consider the following two example entries in an observation log:

1. The student sitting in the dining hall enjoys his greasy, oil-soaked pizza. He is clearly oblivious of the calorie content and damage it may do to his body.
2. The student sits in the dining hall. As he eats his piece of pizza, which drips oil, he says to a friend, "This pizza is good."

The first entry is biased and demonstrates judgment about the event. First, the observer makes assumptions about the internal state of the student when she writes "enjoys" and "clearly oblivious to the calorie content." From an observer's standpoint, there is no way of ascertaining what the student may or may not know about pizza's nutritional value nor how much the student enjoys the pizza. The second entry provides only the details and facts that are observable.

Observations	Thoughts
The student sits in the dining hall. As he eats his piece of pizza, which drips oil, he says to a friend, "This pizza is good."	It seems like the student really enjoys the high-calorie content pizza.
I observed cash register #1 for 15 minutes. During that time 22 students paid for meals. Of those 22 students, 15 grabbed a candy bar or granola bar. 3 of the 22 students had a piece of fruit on their plate.	Fruit is less accessible than candy bars (it is further back in the dining court). Is this why more students are reaching for candy bars?

FIGURE 3 Two Sample Entries From a Double-Entry Notebook.

To avoid bias in your observations, you can use something called a "double-entry notebook." This is a type of observation log that encourages you to separate your observations (the facts) from your feelings and judgments about the facts.

Observations are only one strategy in collecting primary research. You may also want to ask people directly about their behaviors, beliefs, or attitudes—and for this you will need to use surveys or interviews.

SURVEYS AND INTERVIEWS: QUESTION CREATION

Sometimes it is very difficult for a researcher to gain all of the necessary information through observations alone. Along with his observations of the dining halls, Derek wanted to know what students ate in a typical day, and so he used a survey to have them keep track of their eating habits. Likewise, Jared wanted to learn about writing and communication in engineering and decided to draw upon expert knowledge by asking experienced individuals within the field.

Interviews and surveys are two ways that you can gather information about people's beliefs or behaviors. With these methods, the information you collect is not firsthand (like an observation) but rather "self-reported" data, or data collected in an indirect manner. William Shadish, Thomas Cook, and Donald Campbell argued that people are inherently biased about how they see the world and may report their own actions in a more favorable way than they may actually behave. Despite the issues in self-reported data, surveys and interviews are an excellent way to gather data for your primary research project.

Survey or Interview?

How do you choose between conducting a survey or an interview? It depends on what kind of information you are looking for. You should use surveys if you want to learn about a general trend in people's opinions, experiences, and behavior. Surveys are particularly useful to find small amounts of information from a wider selection of people in the hopes of making a general claim. Interviews are best used when you want to learn detailed information from a few specific people. Interviews are also particularly useful if you want to interview experts about their opinions, as Jared did. In sum, use interviews to gain details from a few people, and surveys to learn general patterns from many people.

Writing Good Questions

One of the greatest challenges in conducting surveys and interviews is writing good questions. As a researcher, you are always trying to eliminate bias, and the questions you ask need to be unbiased and clear. Here are some suggestions on writing good questions:

Ask About One Thing at a Time

A poorly written question can contain multiple questions, which can confuse participants or lead them to answer only part of the question you are asking. This is called a "double-barreled question" in journalism. The following questions are taken from Jared's research:

> Poor question: What kinds of problems are being faced in the field today and where do you see the search for solutions to these problems going?
>
> Revised question #1: What kinds of problems are being faced in the field today?
>
> Revised question #2: Where do you see the search for solutions to these problems going?

Avoid Leading Questions

A leading question is one where you prompt the participant to respond in a particular way, which can create bias in the answers given:

> Leading question: The economy is clearly in a crisis, wouldn't you agree?
> Revised question: Do you believe the economy is currently in a crisis? Why or why not?

Understand When to Use Open and Closed Questions

Closed questions, or questions that have yes/no or other limited responses, should be used in surveys. However, avoid these kinds of questions in interviews because they discourage the interviewee from going into depth. The question sample above, "Do you believe the economy currently is in a crisis?" could be answered with a simple yes or no, which could keep a participant from talking more about the issue. The "why or why not?" portion of the question asks the participant to elaborate. On a survey, the question "Do you believe the economy currently is in a crisis?" is a useful question because you can easily count the number of yes and no answers and make a general claim about participant responses.

Write Clear Questions

When you write questions, make sure they are clear, concise, and to the point. Questions that are too long, use unfamiliar vocabulary, or are unclear may confuse participants and you will not get quality responses.

Now that question creation has been addressed, we will next examine specific considerations for interviews and surveys.

INTERVIEWS

Interviews, or question and answer sessions with one or more people, are an excellent way to learn in-depth information from a person for your primary research project. This section presents information on how to conduct a successful interview, including choosing the right person, ways of interviewing, recording your interview, interview locations, and transcribing your interview.

Choosing the Right Person

One of the keys to a successful interview is choosing the right person to interview. Think about whom you would like to interview and whom you might know. Do not be afraid to ask people you do not know for interviews. When asking, simply tell them what the interview will be about, what the interview is for, and how much time it will take. Jared used his Purdue University connection to locate both of the individuals that he ended up interviewing—an advanced Purdue student and a Purdue alum working in an Engineering firm.

Face-to-Face and Virtual Interviews

When interviewing, you have a choice of conducting a traditional, face-to-face interview or an interview using technology over the Internet. Face-to-face interviews have the strength that you can ask follow-up questions and use non-verbal communication to your advantage. Individuals are able to say much more in a face-to-face interview than in an email, so you will get more information from a face-to-face interview. However, the Internet provides a host of new possibilities when it comes to interviewing people at a distance. You may choose to do an email interview, where you send questions and ask the person to respond. You may also choose to use a video or audio conferencing program to talk with the person virtually. If you are choosing any Internet-based option, make sure you have a way of recording the interview. You may also use a chat or instant messaging program to interview your participant—the benefit of this is that you can ask follow-up questions during the interview and the interview is already transcribed for you. Because one of his interviewees lived several hours away, Jared chose to interview the Purdue student face-to-face and the Purdue alum via email.

Finding a Suitable Location

If you are conducting an in-person interview, it is essential that you find a quiet place for your interview. Many universities have quiet study rooms that can be reserved (often found in the university library). Do not try to interview someone in a coffee shop, dining hall, or other loud area, as it is difficult to focus and get a clear recording.

Recording Interviews

One way of eliminating bias in your research is to record your interviews rather than rely on your memory. Recording interviews allows you to directly quote the individual and re-read the interview when you are writing. It is recommended that you have two recording devices for the interview in case one recording device fails. Most computers, MP3 players, and even cell phones come with recording equipment built in. Many universities also offer equipment that students can check out and use, including computers and recorders. Before you record any interview, be sure that you have permission from your participant.

Transcribing Your Interview

Once your interview is over, you will need to transcribe your interview to prepare it for analysis. The term transcribing means creating a written record that is exactly what was said—i.e. typing up your interviews. If you have conducted an email or chat interview, you already have a transcription and can move on to your analysis stage.

SURVEYS

Other than the fact that they both involve asking people questions, interviews and surveys are quite different data collection methods. Creating a survey may seem easy at first, but developing a quality survey can be quite challenging. When conducting a survey, you need to focus on the following areas: survey creation, survey testing, survey sampling, and distributing your survey.

Survey Creation: Length and Types of Questions

One of the keys to creating a successful survey is to keep your survey short and focused. Participants are unlikely to fill out a survey that is lengthy, and you'll have a more difficult time during your analysis if your survey contains too many questions. In most cases, you want your survey to be something that can be filled out within a few minutes. The target length of the survey also depends on how you will distribute the survey. If you are giving your survey to other students in your dorm or classes, they will have more time to complete the survey. Therefore, five to ten minutes to complete the survey is reasonable. If you are asking students as they are walking to class to fill out your survey, keep it limited to several questions that can be answered in thirty seconds or less. Derek's survey took about ten minutes and asked students to describe what they ate for a day, along with some demographic information like class level and gender.

Use closed questions to your advantage when creating your survey. A closed question is any set of questions that gives a limited amount of choices (yes/no, a 1–5 scale, choose the statement that best describes you). When creating closed questions, be sure that you are accounting for all reasonable answers in your question creation. For example, asking someone "Do you believe you eat healthy?" and providing them only "yes" and "no" options means that a "neutral" or "undecided" option does not exist, even though the survey respondent may not feel strongly either way. Therefore, on closed questions you may find it helpful to include an "other" category where participants can fill in an answer. It is also a good idea to have a few open-ended questions where participants can elaborate on certain points or earlier responses. However, open-ended questions take much longer to fill out than closed questions.

Survey Creation: Testing Your Survey

To make sure your survey is an appropriate length and that your questions are clear, you can "pilot test" your survey. Prior to administering your survey on a larger scale, ask several classmates or friends to fill it out and give you feedback on the survey. Keep track of how long the survey takes to complete. Ask them if the questions are clear and make sense. Look at their answers to see if the answers match what you wanted to learn. You can revise your survey questions and the length of your survey as necessary.

Sampling and Access to Survey Populations

"Sampling" is a term used within survey research to describe the subset of people that are included in your study. Derek's first research question was: "Are students' eating habits at Purdue University healthy or unhealthy?" Because it was impossible for Derek to survey all 38,000 students on Purdue's campus, he had to choose a representative sample of students. Derek chose to survey students who lived in the dorms because of the wide variety of student class levels and majors in the dorms and his easy access to this group. By making this choice, however, he did not account for commuter students, graduate students, or those who live off campus. As Derek's case demonstrates, it is very challenging to get a truly representative sample.

Part of the reason that sampling is a challenge is that you may find difficulty in finding enough people to take your survey. In thinking about how to get people to take your survey, consider both your everyday surroundings and also technological solutions. Derek had access to many students in the dorms, but he also considered surveying students in his classes in order to reach as many people as possible. Another possibility is to conduct an online survey. Online surveys greatly increase your access to different kinds of people from across the globe, but may decrease your chances of having a high survey response rate. An email or private message survey request is more likely to be ignored due to the impersonal quality and high volume of emails most people receive.

ANALYZING AND WRITING ABOUT PRIMARY RESEARCH

Once you collect primary research data, you will need to analyze what you have found so that you can write about it. The purpose of analyzing your data is to look at what you collected (survey responses, interview answers to questions, observations) and to create a cohesive, systematic interpretation to help answer your research question or examine the validity of your hypothesis.

When you are analyzing and presenting your findings, remember to work to eliminate bias by being truthful and as accurate as possible about what you found, even if it differs from what you expected to find. You should see your data as sources of information, just like sources you find in the library, and you should work to represent them accurately.

The following are suggestions for analyzing different types of data.

Observations

If you've counted anything you were observing, you can simply add up what you counted and report the results. If you've collected descriptions using a double-entry notebook, you might work to write thick descriptions of what you observed into your writing. This could include descriptions of the scene, behaviors you observed, and your overall conclusions about events. Be sure that your readers are clear on what were your actual observations versus your thoughts or interpretations of those observations.

Interviews

If you've interviewed one or two people, then you can use your summary, paraphrasing, and quotation skills to help you accurately describe what was said in the interview. Just like in secondary research when working with sources, you should introduce your interviewees and choose clear and relevant quotes from the interviews to use in your writing. An easy way to find the important information in an interview is to print out your transcription and take a highlighter and mark the important parts that you might use in your paper. If you have conducted a large number of interviews, it will be helpful for you to create a spreadsheet of responses to each question and compare the responses, choosing representative answers for each area you want to describe.

Surveys

Surveys can contain quantitative (numerical) and qualitative (written answers/descriptions) data. Quantitative data can be analyzed using a spreadsheet program like Microsoft Excel to calculate the mean (average) answer or to calculate the percentage of people who responded in a certain way. You can display this information in a chart or a graph and also describe it in writing in your paper. If you have qualitative responses, you might choose to group them into categories and/or you may choose to quote several representative responses.

WRITING ABOUT PRIMARY RESEARCH

In formal research writing in a variety of fields, it is common for research to be presented in the following format: introduction/background; methods; results; discussions; conclusion. Not all first year writing classes will require such an organizational structure, although it is likely that you will be required to present many of these elements in your paper. Because of this, the next section examines each of these in depth.

Introduction (Review of Literature)

The purpose of an introduction and review of literature in a research paper is to provide readers with information that helps them understand the context, purpose, and relevancy of your research. The introduction is where you provide most of your background (library) research that you did earlier in the process. You can include articles, statistics, research studies, and quotes that are pertinent to the issues at hand. A second purpose in an introduction is to establish your own credibility (ethos) as a writer by showing that you have researched your topic thoroughly. This kind of background discussion is required in nearly every field of inquiry when presenting research in oral or written formats.

Derek provided information from the Food and Drug Administration on healthy eating and national statistics about eating habits as part of his background information. He also made the case for healthy eating on campus to show relevancy:

> Currently Americans are more overweight than ever. This is coming at a huge cost to the economy and government. If current trends in increasing rates of overweight and obesity continue it is likely that this generation will be the first one to live shorter lives than their parents did. Looking at the habits of university students is a good way to see how a new generation behaves when they are living out on their own for the first time.

Describing What You Did (Methods)

When writing, you need to provide enough information to your readers about your primary research process for them to understand what you collected and how you collected it. In formal research papers, this is often called a methods section. Providing information on your study methods also adds to your credibility as a writer. For surveys, your methods would include describing who you surveyed, how many surveys you collected, decisions you made about your survey sample, and relevant demographic information about your participants (age, class level, major). For interviews, introduce whom you interviewed and any other relevant information about interviewees such as their career or expertise area. For observations, list the locations and times you observed and how you recorded your observations (i.e. double-entry notebook). For all data types, you should describe how you analyzed your data.

The following is a sample from Jared about his participants:

> In order to gain a better understanding of the discourse community in environmental and resource engineering, I interviewed Anne Dare, a senior in environmental and natural resource engineering, and Alyson Keaton an alumnus of Purdue University. Alyson is a current employee of the Natural Resource Conservation Service (NRCS), which is a division of the United States Department of Agriculture (USDA).

Here is a sample from Derek's methods section:

> I conducted a survey so that I could find out what students at Purdue actually eat on a typical day. I handed out surveys asking students to record what they ate for a day . . . I received 29 back and averaged the results based on average number of servings from each food group on the old food guide pyramid. The group included students from the freshman to the graduate level and had 8 women and 21 men respond.

Describing Your Study Findings (Results)

In a formal research paper, the results section is where you describe what you found. The results section can include charts, graphs, lists, direct quotes, and overviews of findings. Readers find it helpful if you are able to provide the information in different formats. For example, if you have any kind of numbers or percentages, you can talk about them in your written description and then present a graph or chart showing them visually. You

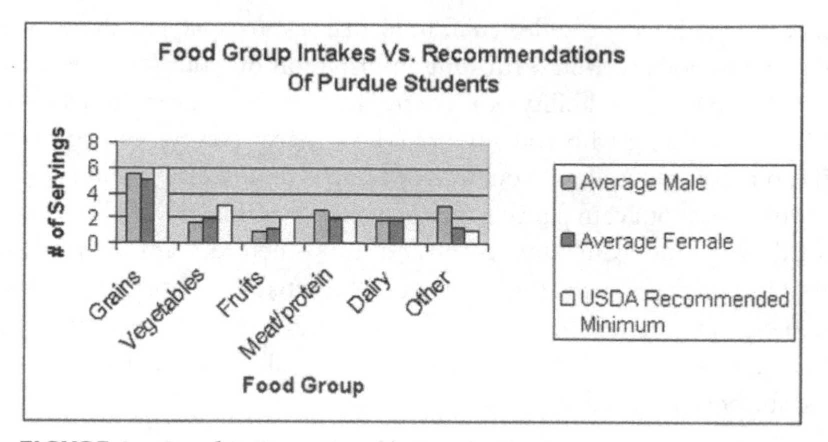

FIGURE 4 Graphic From Derek's Results Section

should provide specific details as supporting evidence to back up your findings. These details can be in the form of direct quotations, numbers, or observations.

Jared describes some of his interview results:

> Alyson also mentioned the need for phone conversation. She stated, "The phone is a large part of my job. I am communicating with other NRCS offices daily to find out the status of our jobs." She needs to be in constant contact in order to insure that everything is running smoothly. This is common with those overseeing projects. In these cases, the wait for a response to an email or a memo can be too long to be effective.

Interpreting What You Learned (Discussion)

In formal research papers, the discussion section presents your own interpretation of your results. This may include what you think the results mean or how they are useful to your larger argument. If you are making a proposal for change or a call to action, this is where you make it. For example, in Derek's project about healthy eating on campus, Derek used his primary research on students' unhealthy eating and observations of the food courts to argue that the campus food courts needed serious changes.

Derek writes, "Make healthy food options the most accessible in every dining hall while making unhealthy foods the least. Put nutrition facts for everything that is served in the dining halls near the food so that students can make more informed decisions on what to eat."

Jared used the individuals he interviewed as informants that helped him learn more about writing in agricultural and biological engineering. He integrated the interviews he conducted with secondary research to form a complete picture of writing and communication in agricultural and biological engineering. He concludes:

> Writing takes so many forms, and it is important to know about all these forms in one way or another. The more forms of writing you can achieve, the more flexible you can be. This ability to be flexible can make all the difference in writing when you are dealing with a field as complex as engineering.

Primary Research and Works Cited or References Pages

The last part of presenting your primary research project is a works cited or references page. In general, since you are working with data you collected yourself, there is no source to cite an external source. Your methods section should describe in detail to the readers how and where the data presented was obtained. However, if you are working with interviews, you can cite these as "personal communication." The MLA and APA handbooks both provide clear listings of how to cite personal communication in a works cited/references page.

CONCLUSION

This essay has presented an overview to three commonly used methods of primary research in first year writing courses: observations, interviews, and surveys. By using these methods, you can learn more about the world around you and craft meaningful written discussions of your findings.

Suggested Resources

For more information on the primary methods of inquiry described here, please see the following sources:

Babbie, Earl. *The Practice of Social Research.* 10th edition. Wadsworth Publishing, 2003. Print.

Creswell, John. *Research Design: Qualitative, Quantitative, and Mixed Methods Approaches.* 3rd ed. Sage publications, 2008. Print.

Fink, Arlene. *How to Conduct Surveys: A Step-by-Step Guide.* 4th ed. Thousand Oaks, CA: Sage Publications, 2008. Print.

Rubin, Herbert and Irene Rubin. *Qualitative Interviewing: The Art of Hearing Data.* 2nd edition. Thousand Oaks, CA: Sage Publications, 2004. Print.

Sanger, Jack. *Compleat Observer? A Field Research Guide to Observation.* New York: Routledge, 1996. Print.

The National Commission for the Protection of Human Subjects of Biomedical and Behavioral Research. *The Belmont Report.* 18 April 1979. Web. <http://ohsr.od.nih.gov/guidelines/belmont.html>.

Works Cited

Babbie, Earl. *The Practice of Social Research.* 10th ed. Belmont, CA: Wadsworth Publishing, 2003. Print.

Creswell, John. *Research Design: Qualitative, Quantitative, and Mixed Methods Approaches.* 3rd ed. Thousand Oaks, CA: Sage Publications, 2008. Print.

Darwin, Charles. *On the Origin of Species by Means of Natural Selection.* New York: L Hurst and Company, No date. Print.

Lauer, Janice and William Asher. *Composition Research: Empirical Designs.* Oxford: Oxford University Press, 1988. Print.

Leavitt, Fred. *Evaluating Scientific Research: Separating Fact from Fiction.* Long Grove, IL: Waveland Press, 2004. Print.

Mead, Margaret. *Growing Up in New Guinea: A Comparative Study of Primitive Education.* New York: Morrow, 1930. Print.

Mill, John Stuart. *John Stuart Mill's Philosophy of Scientific Method.* Ernest Nagel, Ed. New York: Hafner Publishing Co, 1950. Print.

Rubin, Herbert and Irene Rubin. *Qualitative Interviewing: The Art of Hearing Data.* 2nd ed. Thousand Oaks, CA: Sage Publications, 2004. Print.

Shadish, William, Thomas Cook and Donald Campbell. *Quasi-Experimentation: Design and Analysis Issues.* Boston, MA: Houghton Mifflin Company, 1979. Print.

The Meaning of Serena Williams

On tennis and black excellence

Claudia Rankine

There is no more exuberant winner than Serena Williams. She leaps into the air, she laughs, she grins, she pumps her fist, she points her index finger to the sky, signaling she's No. 1. Her joy is palpable. It brings me to my feet, and I grin right back at her, as if I've won something, too. Perhaps I have.

There is a belief among some African-Americans that to defeat racism, they have to work harder, be smarter, be *better*. Only after they give 150 percent will white Americans recognize black excellence for what it is. But of course, once recognized, black excellence is then supposed to perform with good manners and forgiveness in the face of any racist slights or attacks. Black excellence is not supposed to be emotional as it pulls itself together to win after questionable calls. And in winning, it's not supposed to swagger, to leap and pump its fist, to state boldly, in the words of Kanye West, "That's what it is, black excellence, baby."

Imagine you have won 21 Grand Slam singles titles, with only four losses in your 25 appearances in the finals. Imagine that you've achieved two "Serena Slams" (four consecutive Slams in a row), the first more than 10 years ago and the second this year. A win at this year's U.S. Open would be

---

your fifth and your first calendar-year Grand Slam—a feat last achieved by Steffi Graf in 1988, when you were just 6 years old. This win would also break your tie for the most U.S. Open titles in the Open era, surpassing the legendary Chris Evert, who herself has called you "a phenomenon that once every hundred years comes around." Imagine that you're the player John McEnroe recently described as "the greatest player, I think, that ever lived." Imagine that, despite all this, there were so many bad calls against you, you were given as one reason video replay needed to be used on the courts. Imagine that you have to contend with critiques of your body that perpetuate racist notions that black women are hypermasculine and unattractive. Imagine being asked to comment at a news conference before a tournament because the president of the Russian Tennis Federation, Shamil Tarpischev, has described you and your sister as "brothers" who are "scary" to look at. Imagine.

The word "win" finds its roots in both joy and grace. Serena's grace comes because she won't be forced into stillness; she won't accept those racist projections onto her body without speaking back; she won't go gently into the white light of victory. Her excellence doesn't mask the struggle it takes to achieve each win. For black people, there is an unspoken script that demands the humble absorption of racist assaults, no matter the scale, because whites need to believe that it's no big deal. But Serena refuses to keep to that script. Somehow, along the way, she made a decision to be excellent while still being Serena. She would feel what she feels in front of everyone, in response to anyone. At Wimbledon this year, for example, in a match against the home favorite Heather Watson, Serena, interrupted during play by the deafening support of Watson, wagged her index finger at the crowd and said, "Don't try me." She will tell an audience or an official that they are disrespectful or unjust, whether she says, simply, "No, no, no" or something much more forceful, as happened at the U.S. Open in 2009, when she told the lineswoman, "I swear to God I am [expletive] going to take this [expletive] ball and shove it down your [expletive] throat." And in doing so, we actually see her. She shows us her joy, her humor and, yes, her rage. She gives us the whole range of what it is to be human, and there are those who can't bear it, who can't tolerate the humanity of an ordinary extraordinary person.

In the essay "Everybody's Protest Novel," James Baldwin wrote, "our humanity is our burden, our life; we need not battle for it; we need only to do what is infinitely more difficult—that is, accept it." To accept the self, its humanity, is to discard the white racist gaze. Serena has freed herself from it. But that doesn't mean she won't be emotional or hurt by challenges to her humanity. It doesn't mean she won't battle for the right to be excellent. There is nothing wrong with Serena, but surely there is something wrong with the expectation that she be "good" while she is achieving greatness. Why should Serena not respond to racism? In whose world should it be answered with good manners? The notable difference between black excellence and white excellence is white excellence is achieved without having to battle racism. Imagine.

Two years ago, recovering from cancer and to celebrate my 50th birthday, I flew from LAX to J.F.K. during Serena's semifinal match at the U.S. Open with the hope of seeing her play in the final. I had just passed through a year when so much was out of my control, and Serena epitomized not so much winning as the pure drive to win. I couldn't quite shake the feeling (I still can't quite shake it) that my body's frailty, not the cancer but the depth of my exhaustion, had been brought on in part by the constant onslaught of racism, whether something as terrible as the killing of Trayvon Martin or something as mundane as the guy who let the door slam in my face. The daily grind of being rendered invisible, or being attacked, whether physically or verbally, for being visible, wears a body down. Serena's strength and focus in the face of the realities we shared oddly consoled me.

That Sunday in Arthur Ashe Stadium at the women's final, though the crowd generally seemed pro-Serena, the man seated next to me was cheering for the formidable tall blonde Victoria Azarenka. I asked him if he was American. "Yes," he said.

"We're at the U.S. Open. Why are you cheering for the player from Belarus?" I asked.

"Oh, I just want the match to be competitive," he said.

After Serena lost the second set, at the opening of the third, I turned to him again, and asked him, no doubt in my own frustration, why he was still cheering for Azarenka. He didn't answer, as was his prerogative. By the time it was clear that Serena was likely to win, his seat had been vacated. I had to admit to myself that in those moments I needed her to win, not just in the pure sense of a fan supporting her player, but to prove something that could never be proven, because if black excellence could cure us of anything, black people—or rather this black person—would be free from needing Serena to win.

"You don't understand me," Serena Williams said with a hint of impatience in her voice. "I'm just about winning." She and I were facing each other on a sofa in her West Palm Beach home this July. She looked at me with wariness as if to say, Not you, too. I wanted to talk about the tennis records that she is presently positioned either to tie or to break and had tried more than once to steer the conversation toward them. But she was clear: "It's not about getting 22 Grand Slams," she insisted. Before winning a calendar-year Grand Slam and matching Steffi Graf's record of 22 Slams, Serena would have to win seven matches and defend her U.S. Open title; *those* were the victories that she was thinking about.

She was wearing an enviable pink jumpsuit with palm trees stamped all over it as if to reflect the trees surrounding her estate. It was a badass outfit, one only someone of her height and figure could rock. She explained to me that she learned not to look ahead too much by looking ahead. As she approached 18 Grand Slam wins in 2014, she said, "I went too crazy. I felt I had to even up with Chris Evert and Martina Navratilova." Instead, she didn't make it past the fourth round at the Australian Open, the second at the French Open or the third at Wimbledon. She tried to change her tactics and focused on getting only to the quarterfinals of the U.S. Open. Make it to the second week and see what happens, she thought. "I started thinking like that, and then I got to 19. Actually I got to 21 just like that, so I'm not thinking about 22." She raised her water bottle to her lips, looking at me over its edge, as if to give me time to think of a different line of questioning.

Three years ago she partnered with the French tennis coach Patrick Mouratoglou, and I've wondered if his coaching has been an antidote to negotiating American racism, a dynamic that informed the coaching of her father, Richard Williams. He didn't want its presence to prevent her and Venus from winning. In his autobiography, *Black and White: The Way I See It,* he describes toughening the girls' "skin" by bringing "busloads of kids from the local schools into Compton to surround the courts while Venus and Serena practiced. I had the kids call them every curse word in the

English language, including 'Nigger,'" he writes. "I paid them to do it and told them to 'do their worst.'" His focus on racism meant that the sisters were engaged in two battles on and off the court. That level of vigilance, I know from my own life, can drain you. It's easier to shut up and pretend it's not happening, as the bitterness and stress build up.

Mouratoglou shifted Serena's focus to records (even if, as she prepares for a Slam, she says she can't allow herself to think about them). Perhaps it's not surprising that she broke her boycott against Indian Wells, where the audience notoriously booed her with racial epithets in 2001, during their partnership. Serena's decisions now seem directed toward building her legacy. Mouratoglou has insisted that she can get to 24 Grand Slams, which is the most won by a single player—Margaret Court —to date. Serena laughed as she recalled one of her earliest conversations with Mouratoglou. She told him: "I'm cool. I want to play tennis. I hate to lose. I want to win. But I don't have numbers in my head." He wouldn't allow that. "Now we are getting numbers in your head," he told her.

I asked how winning felt for her. I was imagining winning as a free space, one where the unconscious racist shenanigans of umpires, or the narratives about her body, her "unnatural" power, her perceived crassness no longer mattered. Unless racism destroyed the moment of winning so completely, as it did at Indian Wells, I thought it had to be the rare space free of all the stresses of black life. But Serena made it clear that she doesn't desire to dissociate from her history and her culture. She understands that even when she's focused only on winning, she is still representing. "I play for me," Serena told me, "but I also play and represent something much greater than me. I embrace that. I love that. I want that. So ultimately, when I am out there on the court, I am playing for me."

Her next possible victory is at the U.S. Open, the major where she has been involved in the most drama—everything from outrageous line calls to probations and fines. Serena admitted to losing her cool in the face of some of what has gone down there. In 2011, for example, a chair umpire, Eva Asderaki, ruled against Serena for yelling "Come on" before a point was completed, and as Serena described it to me, she "clutched her pearls" and told Asderaki not to look at her. But she said in recent years she finally felt embraced by the crowd. "No more incidents?" I asked. Before she could answer, we both laughed, because of course it's not wholly in her control.

Then suddenly Serena stopped. "I don't want any incidents there," she said. "But I'm always going to be myself. If anything happens, I'm always going to be myself, true to myself."

I'm counting on it, I thought. Because just as important to me as her victories is her willingness to be an emotionally complete person while also being black. She wins, yes, but she also loses it. She jokes around, gets angry, is frustrated or joyous, and on and on. She is fearlessly on the side of Serena, in a culture that that has responded to living while black with death.

This July, the London School of Marketing (L.S.M.) released its list of the most marketable sports stars, which included only two women in its Top 20: Maria Sharapova and Serena Williams. They were ranked 12th and 20th. Despite decisively trailing Serena on the tennis court (Serena leads in their head-to-head matchups 18-2, and has 21 majors and 247 weeks at No. 1 to Sharapova's five majors and 21 weeks at number 1), Sharapova has a financial advantage off the court. This month Forbes listed her as the highest-paid female athlete, worth more than $29 million to Serena's $24 million.

When I asked Chris Evert about the L.S.M. list, she said, "I think the corporate world still loves the good-looking blond girls." It's a preference Evert benefited from in her own illustrious career. I suggested that this had to do with race. Serena, on occasion, has herself been a blonde. But of course, for millions of consumers, possibly not the right kind of blonde. "Maria was very aware of business and becoming a businesswoman at a much younger stage," Evert told me, adding, "She works hard." She also suggested that any demonstration of corporate preference is about a certain "type" of look or image, not whiteness in general. When I asked Evert what she made of Eugenie Bouchard, the tall, blond Canadian who has yet to really distinguish herself in the sport, being named the world's most marketable athlete by the British magazine *SportsPro* this spring, she said, with a laugh, "Well, there you have it." I took her statement to be perhaps a moment of agreement that Serena probably could not work her way to Sharapova's spot on Forbes's list.

"If they want to market someone who is white and blond, that's their choice," Serena told me when I asked her about her ranking. Her impatience had returned, but I wasn't sure if it was with me, the list or both. "I have a lot of partners who are very happy to work with me." JPMorgan Chase, Wilson Sporting Goods, Pepsi and Nike are among the partners she was referring to. "I can't sit here and say I should be higher on the list because I have won more." As for Sharapova, her nonrival rival, Serena was diplomatic: "I'm happy for her, because she worked hard, too. There is enough at the table for everyone."

There is another, perhaps more important, discussion to be had about what it means to be chosen by global corporations. It has to do with who is worthy, who is desirable, who is associated with the good life. As long as the white imagination markets itself by equating whiteness and blondness with aspirational living, stereotypes will remain fixed in place. Even though Serena is the best, even though she wins more Slams than anyone else, she is only superficially allowed to embody that in our culture, at least the marketable one.

But Serena was less interested in the ramifications involved in being chosen, since she had no power in this arena, and more interested in understanding her role in relation to those who came before her: "We have to be thankful, and we also have to be positive about it so the next black person can be No. 1 on that list," she told me. "Maybe it was not meant to be me. Maybe it's meant to be the next person to be amazing, and I'm just opening the door. Zina Garrison, Althea Gibson, Arthur Ashe and Venus opened so many doors for me. I'm just opening the next door for the next person."

I was moved by Serena's positioning herself in relation to other African-Americans. A crucial component of white privilege is the idea that your accomplishments can be, have been, achieved on your own. The private clubs that housed the tennis courts remained closed to minorities well into the second half of the 20th century. Serena reminded me that in addition to being a phenomenon, she has come out of a long line of African-Americans who battled for the right to be excellent in such a space that attached its value to its whiteness and worked overtime to keep it segregated.

Serena's excellence comes with the ability to imagine herself achieving a new kind of history for all of us. As long as she remains healthy, she will most likely tie and eventually pass Graf's 22 majors, regardless of what happens at the U.S. Open this year. I want Serena to win, but I know better than to think her winning can end something she didn't start. But Serena is providing a new script, one in which winning doesn't carry the burden of curing racism, in which we win just to win—knowing that it is simply her excellence, baby.

Correction: September 13, 2015

An article on Aug. 30 about Serena Williams misidentified the tennis official she confronted at the U.S. Open in 2009 after she was called for a foot fault. The official was a lineswoman, not a chair umpire.

Greg Allen

Jody Santos

College Writing

7 March 2015

Disney: Sexist and Racist Since 1937

A family gathers together, pulls the hot, buttery popcorn out of the microwave and pours it into a bowl. They grab warm blankets and get cuddled up on the couch. The children's eyes are wide as ever as the father pops *Peter Pan* into the VCR. The family is in for a magical night of entertainment as the Disney production appears on the screen. However, what else is entering the minds of these children? When the viewer digs a little deeper, Disney becomes a monster. Its productions are absurdly racist and sexist across the board. Many criticized Disney for some of its racism and sexism, and some changes were made, but there is still an underlying element in each of its films. Many would argue that with the productions of *Pocahontas, Mulan, Princess and the Frog,* and more, Disney entered a post-racial and post-sexist era. However, so many of the stereotypes still exist—even in those films. Children that absorb these movies are affected by the images presented, and almost nothing has changed since some of the first Disney productions.

According to the documentary, *Mickey Mouse Monopoly*, in some of the earliest Disney movies like *Fantasia* (1940) and *Snow White and the Seven Dwarves* (1937), there is a very distinct image of females that is presented. The common traits include long, dashing eyelashes and very skinny waists. The bodies are highly sexualized, and the behaviors of the females are extremely seductive. Overtime, however, nothing has changed. As the years carry on, the traits remain the same. These traits are seen in *Bambi* (1942), *The Jungle Book* (1967), *The Little Mermaid* (1989), *Beauty and the Beast* (1991), *Aladdin* (1992), *Pocahontas* (1995), *Hercules* (1997), *Frozen* (2013) and many more. One example of the seductiveness is seen in *Aladdin.* There is a scene in which Jasmine uses her body and seduces a man as a distraction for Aladdin to accomplish a task. This is dangerous for girls because it teaches them that they can use their bodies to get what they want. Perhaps the worst part is, the images do not even come close to resembling real females. As the images of females repeat themselves throughout the films, young girls get the idea that they should look just like the women in the movies. If a girl is normal, there is a high chance she becomes uncomfortable in her own skin because of the extremely beautiful and unrealistic females that are in the Disney films (*Mickey Mouse Monopoly*). Something else that has to do with body image is the evil person in Disney films. The "bad person" always seems to be unattractive. This is true in *Snow White and the Seven Dwarfs* where the witch is short, round, and has a very different face than Snow White or any "good person" in the movie. It is also seen in *The Little Mermaid.* Ursala is larger and has a blemish on her face. This idea is bad for girls because if a girl has a blemish or is a little larger, they receive the message that they aren't as good as a skinny girl with no blemishes.

However, the images do not just effect young girls. Males are highly affected by gender qualities in Disney movies as well. In most films, the men are brave, adventurous, unemotional, and physically strong (Collier-

Meek, 559). In *Tarzan,* for example, he is extremely strong and he is the hero who kills the leopard and protects Jane, the innocent and helpless female. In *Beauty and the Beast*, the beast is assertive and dominant over Belle. According to *Mickey Mouse Monopoly* and Dr. Carolyn Newburger, a psychologist at Harvard University, he screams at her, imprisons her, refuses to feed her, and throws her around like a rag doll. The beast is abusive and controlling, but in the end he still gets the beautiful girl. This is perhaps the most dangerous message because it shows that men can attain what they want by being in control and abusing a woman (*Mickey Mouse Monopoly*).

Another issue with gender and Disney is that no matter how independent or strong a woman may be, she still always needs to be rescued by a male character. The females are always the ones that seem to find trouble, and the males always come to the rescue. One example of this is seen in *The Hunchback of Notre Dame*. When the woman is tied to the pole and is about to be burned, the male comes swinging in on a rope to save her. When children see this they begin to play the roles. According to Allison Wilson in *Mickey Mouse Monopoly*, there were children playing on a playground and one girl was laying against a fence crying for help, and all the boys were going to rescue her (*Mickey Mouse Monopoly*).

Disney received a standing ovation after producing the movie *Pocahontas* because a Native American was added to the previously Caucasian-dominated princess series. However, the Native American culture is still depicted very unfairly. Throughout *Pocahontas,* the Natives are referred to on nearly every occasion as "savages" by the Englishmen.

Allen 4

It is a word that indicates uncivilized, animal-like people that have no right to live by their own standards. When children see this movie and see the way Native Americans are referred to, they get the idea shoved into their heads that Native Americans are not people, but animals that do not belong. There is a similar portrayal of this in *Peter Pan.* When the kids in the movie are introduced to the Native Americans, the Natives are sitting with their legs crossed, singing songs, running, jumping, and yelling while repeatedly hitting their hand against their mouth to create the stereotypical Native American sound. For many young viewers these films are the only time they have seen Native American people so their only perception is the untrue, savage behavior that is shown in the movies (*Mickey Mouse Monopoly*).

Another race that is neglected throughout Disney productions is the Latino race. In Disney films there are hardly any Latino characters, and when there are, they are animals, play a minor role, and fit the typical stereotypes of a Mexican or Latin person. Two examples of this are seen in *Oliver and Company* and in *Lady and the Tramp* with the chihuahuas. In these movies, the dogs do things that they aren't supposed to do. In *Oliver and Company,* Alonzo steals a car. The dogs also have heavy accents in the movies and they represent something that nobody wants. They are filthy, dirty "things" that nobody would even ponder wanting something to do with (*Mickey Mouse Monopoly*). African Americans are also highly oppressed in Disney films. They also always seem to be represented by animals. They are crows, or monkeys, or, in *The Lion King,* hyenas. There is also a very unfair, stereotypical representation of African Americans. In *Dumbo*, the crows have a slowed down, slurred speech. In *The Jungle*

Allen 5

Book, there are monkeys that sound and dance like a stereotypical black person. They sing a song about how they want to be like men, but they will never be able to accomplish that. *Tarzan,* which takes place in Africa, does not represent black people at all. Lastly, in *The Lion King,* the hyenas also sound like a stereotypical black person and the hyenas are the bad guys. They do bad things to Simba and try to hurt him. This representation is so glaring that one little boy was at a playground and he ran over to his mother and said, "Mommy, Mommy, it's the hyenas!" The mother looked up to see African American children playing on the swing set. However, she admitted that when she put her head down and just listened to the boys playing, they sounded exactly like the hyenas in *The Lion King.* This is dangerous for kids because when Latinos and African Americans are represented doing bad or illegal things in movies, Caucasian children become afraid of those races in real life. It is also dangerous to Latino and African American children because they see these images and believe that they should act in a similar manner (*Mickey Mouse Monopoly*).

In a study conducted by Sherri Burr, a law professor at the University of New Mexico, children were asked how often they saw their race on television and the roles that their race played. The results were shocking. 58 percent of children said that they saw white people having a lot of money. Only eight percent of minorities said they saw their races with a substantial amount of money. 71 percent of white children said they saw whites on television very often, where just 42 percent of African American children saw their race on television (Burr). Many people, like Neal Gabler of *The Los Angeles Times,* argue that as of the mid-2000s, this has come to an end. In 2009, the Disney production, *The Princess and the Frog* was released, and the movie featured an African American princess. Gabler says, "Even before it opens later this week, Disney's new animated feature, 'The Princess and the Frog,' is already considered something of a cultural and animation landmark." The author goes on to argue that Walt Disney himself was the man who brought all the racism to Disney, but now that he has passed, we have entered a post-racial era (Gabler). However, Gabler's argument seems invalid as many other experts would argue that just because the movie features a black princess, it does not mean the film doesn't have its flaws. In a *The New York Times* article by Brooks Barnes, he states, "Disney obviously does not think a black man is worthy of the title 'prince'." He supports the quote by saying that the prince in the film has hair and features that are clearly non-black, and his skin is very fair (Barnes). Another interesting observation is that a black princess falls for a black prince. Of course Disney is not going to make an interracial relationship. There is one interracial relationship in Disney which is between Pocahontas and John Smith, but that movie is based off of a true story so Disney was forced to make the relationship. It is also untrue in the sense that Pocahontas actually married John Rolfe.

It is tough to argue that Disney is perhaps the greatest form of magical and fantasy-like entertainment for children and families. However, the underlying qualities of Disney's films are vicious. Children absorb the messages in the movies and get ideas and thoughts put into their brains about society that are not true. There has also been an extreme lack of progress for Disney over the years despite the criticism it has received.

Even after the movie *The Princess and the Frog,* Disney went back to its old ways with the 2013 production of *Frozen.* In the film every character is white, the princesses are still skinny and abnormally beautiful, and they still need to be saved by males at different times throughout the movie. For example, when they are running away from the wolves, the male does all the work to escape the chasing animals. The males in the movie are still adventurous, physically strong, and unemotional—all characteristics of males in past films from decades ago. Disney is a corrupt company, and its films are still portraying the same negative messages to children. A change needs to be made if people in today's society want racism and sexism to end. Disney movies are the first thing that children see in life, and if the films are giving negative signals to those children, nothing in society is going to change.

Works Cited

Barnes, Brooks. “Her Prince Has Come. Critics, Too.” *The New York Times* 29 May 2009: Web.

Burr, Sherry. “Television and Societal Effects: An Analysis of Media Images of African-Americans in Historical Context.” Racism.org. Web. 1 Mar. 2015.

Collier-Meek, Mellissa, Descartes, Lara, England, Dawn. “Gender Role Portrayal and the Disney Princesses.” Springer Science and Business Media, LLC. 10 February 2011. Web.

Gabler, Neal. “Walt Disney—Prince or Toad.” *The Los Angeles Times* 22 November 2009: Web.

Picker, Miguel. *Mickey Mouse Monopoly.* 2001. Film.

Shuman 1

Josh Shuman

Professor Lartigue

College Writing 1:00

Biases About Language

Throughout history people have tried to discriminate others based on how they speak. People use this to attack the speaker's arguments without actually proving them wrong. When people discriminate against others for how they speak there is an underlying reason which could be racism, misogyny, or many others. Some people who face this discrimination are people with different regional accents, people with nonnative accents, people with speech impediments, people who speak with an African American vernacular, and women who speak with up talk and vocal fry. Each of these ways of speaking carries different negative connotations. People with strong regional accents are often viewed as uneducated and too informal, while people with nonnative accents are viewed as lazy, stupid, and non-compliant. Speakers who have speech impediments are looked as less intelligent and forced to accommodate to the majority of those without speech impediments. Those who speak with an African American vernacular are believed to be stupid and uneducated. Women who speak with up talk and vocal fry are viewed as immature, stupid, and are not taken seriously. Since these people deviate from a neutral American accent, they get mistreated even though there is no link between how one speaks and their intellect. Additionally, discriminating against people for how they speak is wrong because how someone speaks depends on where they grew up, the way their parents speak, and physiological patterns.

A strong regional accent doesn't mean that someone is speaking incorrect English. Unfortunately, there are many people who think that those with different regional accents are uneducated and sound like fools. However, there is no link between how someone speaks and their intellect. Even if these people are more working class people and less educated it does not make them inferior to those who speak with an average American accent. In fact, Professor of Linguistics Dr. Dennis R. Preston asserts that this myth "runs deep, strong and true". Since people have a more neutral American accent are usually of higher status, they force others to comply with how they speak. Anyone who deviates is accused of speaking incorrect English. For example, many people view a southern accent as incorrect since they have a slower way of speaking, different pronunciations, and different slang. Dr. Preston found that even southerners believe their accent isn't correct English. They do enjoy their accent more as they show their regional pride ("They Speak Really Bad English down South and in New York City"). Interestingly enough, Saumya Viashampayan who writes for the *Wall Street Journal* cites a George Mason University study in which they found people believed that a British accent is more intelligent than a Southern accent (qtd. in "When an Accent Gets in the Way of a Job"). This sort of dividing can cause hatred for people one doesn't even know. It also causes people who have these heavier accents to be discriminated in society and the work place. This forces them to change the way they speak which can cause great psychological damage as they try to measure up to society's status quo.

Besides regional accents, those with nonnative accents of English face great obstacles daily based on how they speak. Raymond Hernandez shows in his article in *The New York Times* how some people have dealt with this discrimination. Carmen Friedman emigrated from Colombia and still struggled with her accent even after 5 years in America. She was fed up and decided to take classes to get rid of her accent. Sadly, her accent was damaging and was hurting her image of herself she didn't "want to feel uncomfortable every time I say something" ("When an Accent Becomes an Issue; Immigrants turn to Speech Classes to Reduce Sting of Bias"). Unfortunately, there are numerous stories of people with nonnative accents facing bias. It has hurt them on job interviews and even in the workplace as Paul Foy of the *Insurance Journal* found that Filipino hospital workers won a case for being discriminated for having an accent and speaking in their language at any time during work ("More Workers Claiming Job Discrimination over Language, Accents"). Not all nonnative accents are treated the same way, though, argues associate professor at The Pennsylvania State University Patreese D. Ingram. Many times it is nonwhite people who face the discrimination. There aren't any records of people with various western European accents getting discriminated against. ("Are Accents One of the Last Acceptable Areas for Discrimination") This shows that the underlying bias is a form of racism and xenophobia. Most don't identify with these people so they expect them to talk differently. This can go even further and people can have the expectation that these people are less intelligent since they can't speak the same way. Consequently, the effects of this discrimination can be psychological, as proven by researchers Meifen Wei, Tsun-Yao Ku, and Kenneth T. Wang; they found there to be positive connections between perceived language discrimination and depression and anxiety. There were also negative connections for perceived language discrimination and life satisfaction and self-esteem ("A Development and Validation of the Perceived Language Discrimination Scale", 348–349). These people feel rejected by society which can cause major damage to their well-being. Companies will benefit with more diversity in the workplace as people exchange experiences and talk with people of different backgrounds; therefore it is in the best interest of both groups to stop the bias against them.

People with speech impediments face great obstacles just trying to communicate on a daily basis. Not to mention the lack of understanding that comes along with their impediment. A common speech impediment is stuttering while speaking. People who stutter usually inherit this and it takes many hours of speech therapy to fix it. Sometimes it can never be fixed since it is a physiological disability. People assume because someone stutters that they aren't intelligent or aren't confident in what they are saying. Reporter for the *New York Times* Richard Perez-Pena talks of the story of Philip Garber Jr. The story shows how teachers can discriminate against students with speech impediments by not allowing them to participate in class because they take up too much time. Two students in the class thought that he didn't take up too much time and his input benefitted the class (*Language Awareness* 517–520). This sends the class a message that they are there to listen to the teacher, not to participate and ask questions, resulting in the students worrying if they can respond quickly enough to the teacher to even ask questions. Additionally, the students with speaking disabilities feel as if their opinions aren't even wanted. They have to write down questions and ask after class. This could result in loss of motivation to participate at all.

A less severe impediment is the use of verbal pauses in one's speech like "uh". This is used in many people's speech. It is usually used while someone is thinking of what to say. While many people dislike these filler words, writer for *Slate* Michael Erard believes the uses of these pauses are important and shouldn't be expelled from speech. These pauses are present in other languages like French, German, and Japanese. Surprisingly, the trend to eliminate them only started in the early 20th century. Many people prefer people who speak with verbal pauses because it shows that it is a genuine response. Many studies have found that the verbal pause lets people know that something important is coming. The added emphasis helps listeners tune in (*Language Awareness,* 126-128). This development shows that there is a reason for these pauses and they actually are more beneficial than no pauses at all. The reasons against are coming from the higher class who believe the average speaker must be wrong since they are less educated.

An African American or black vernacular is often associated with being less intelligent and lazy. This sort of assumption has hurt many in the workplace and in school. Sociolinguist professor at North Carolina State University Walt Wolfram talks of the "linguistic inferiority principle" which says the accent of the socially lower class people will be viewed as inferior to other accents (Wolfram, 104). People argue that the use of multiple negatives in black vernacular is wrong since it doesn't logically make sense. However, logic doesn't apply to language and communication. These multiple negatives are also present in older English, French and Spanish so this shows that there is no basis of saying that this is an incorrect way to speak ("Myth 14: Double Negatives are Illogical"). There are many other cases of people trying to punch holes in this vernacular which are proven wrong. This sort of indoctrinated belief has been spread largely due to racial discrimination. Since African Americans have been in the lower social class in America since they arrived, the assumption that they speak incorrectly has stuck. Professor of legal analysis and writing and race and the law William Y. Chin has found that the bias against them in the classroom as well. The teachers believe this dialect is inappropriate for class and they are called on less because of it. The discrimination in the classroom spreads further as they get worse recommendations and put on slower learning tracks ("Linguistic Profiling In Education: How Accent Bias Denies Equal Educational Opportunities To Students Of Color"). This sort of bias can cause damage to the student's life as they try to progress in their education. If their education is hurt than their prospect for a job will hurt too. This causes a cycle that can be passed down if the students are constantly limited in their educational opportunities.

Women face great discrimination in the work environment if they speak with up talk or vocal fry. Up talk is when speakers bring their voice higher up at the end of the sentence, almost making everything sound like a question. Whereas, vocal fry is when the speaker begins to bring their voice down towards the end of the sentence causing their voice to crackle as it goes deeper with less emphasis on each word. Writer James Gorman talks of the various uses of up talk. He found that up talk is a sign that the speaker is not done speaking. Up talk is used to question the listener and keep them engaged in the conversation. Gorman talks about other uses of up talk as he cites linguist Cynthia Gorman. She did a study on college sorority members in Texas. She found that the use of it was to be more inclusive and connect people to the conversation (*Language Awareness,* 169-172). This shows up talk has a direct use and developed for better communication. Women who speak with up talk are accused of being overly feminine, submissive, and stupid. Vocal fry is another way women are discriminated for how they speak. This is a much deeper and creakier voice. Vocal fry is called too masculine and said to make the speaker sound disinterested. Journalist Jessica Grose was receiving complaints for her voice on a *Slate* podcast. She then hired a vocal coach to help her since she didn't want it to affect her job. This caused psychological distress too. She thought about her voice every time she spoke when before that she never even considered it ("From Upspeak to Vocal Fry: Are We 'Policing' Young Women's Voices?"). The policing of women's speech is not equal to the policing males. Jane Kelly of *UVA Today* found that there are highly distinguished males who use this vocal fry. Famous linguist Noam Chomsky and NPR podcast host Ira Glass both use a deep creaky voice ("What's In a Voice? The Debate Over 'Vocal Fry' And What It Means For Women"). This sort of discrimination shows there may be an underlying feeling of misogyny associated with the hatred for how women speak. The reasons for the discrimination could be the myth that women can't be speaking correctly since they aren't on top of society like men.

In conclusion, the discrimination of people based on how they speak is wrong and damaging to society. The discrimination has no factual evidence to back up that there is an incorrect way to speak English. Meaning their discrimination is usually founded on some other hatred of the person like misogyny or racism. As a result, the bias against these people can cause great psychological distress and hold them back in school and work. The more this discrimination is continued the more it will be accepted as right and passed down generations. Thus continuing the cycle of hatred towards people who behave differently.

Works Cited

Chin, William Y. "Linguistic Profiling in Education: How Accent Bias Denies Equal Educational Opportunities to Students of Color." *The Scholar* 12:335 (n.d.): 355–384. Web. 24 Nov. 2015.

Eschholz, Paul, Alfred Rosa, and Virginia Clark. *Language Awareness 11th edition.* New York: Bedford/St. Martin's, 2013. Print.

Foy, Paul. "More Workers Claiming Job Discrimination Over Language, Accents." *InsuranceJournal.com*. Wells Media Group, Inc. 4 Dec. 2012. Web. 24 Nov. 2014.

Grosse, Jessica, Penny Eckert, and Susan Sankin. "From Upspeak to Vocal Fry: Are We 'Policing' Young Women's Voices?" *NPR.org*. NPR. 23 July 2015. Web. 24 Nov. 2015.

Hernandez, Raymond. "When an Accent Becomes an Issue; Immigrants Turn to Speech Class to Reduce Sting of Bias." *NYTimes.com*. The New York Times Company.
2 March 1993. Web. 24 Nov. 2015.

Ingram, Patreese D. "Are Accents One of the Last Acceptable Areas for Discrimination?" *Commentary* 47.1 (2009): n. pag. *Journal of Extension.* Web. 24 Nov. 2015.

Kelly, Jane. "What's in a Voice? The Debate Over 'Vocal Fry' and What it Means for Women." *News.virginia.edu.* University of Virginia. 12 Aug. 2015. Web. 24 Nov. 2015.

Preston, Dennis R. "Do You Speak American?" *Language Prejudice*. PBS, 2005. Web. 24 Nov. 2015

Shuman 9

Trudgill, Peter, Ray Harlow, Jean Aitchison, Anthony Lodge, Edward Carney, Lars-Gunnar Andersson, James Milroy, Michael Montgomery, Winifred Bauer, Howard Giles, Nancy Niedzielski, Lesley Milroy, Walt Wolfram, Jenny Cheshire, J.K. Chambers, Laurie Bauer, Dennis R. Preston, Peter Roach, Nicholas Evans, John H. Esling, and John Algeo. *Language Myths*. London: Penguin Books, 1998. Print.

Vaishampayan, Saumya. "When an Accent Gets in the Way of a Job" *blog.wsj.com.* Dow Jones & Company, Inc. 6 Sept. 2012. Web. 24 Nov. 2015.

Wei, Meifen, Kenneth T. Wang, and Tsun-Yao Ku. "A Development and Validation of the Perceived Language Discrimination Scale." *Cultural Diversity and Ethnic Minority Psychology* 18.4 (2012): 340–351. *PsycARTICLES*. Web. 24 Nov. 2015.

PART 4
Writerly Orientation

Shitty First Drafts

Anne Lamott from *Bird by Bird*

Now, practically even better news than that of short assignments is the idea of shitty first drafts. All good writers write them. This is how they end up with good second drafts and terrific third drafts. People tend to look at successful writers who are getting their books published and maybe even doing well financially and think that they sit down at their desks every morning feeling like a million dollars, feeling great about who they are and how much talent they have and what a great story they have to tell; that they take in a few deep breaths, push back their sleeves, roll their necks a few times to get all the cricks out, and dive in, typing fully formed passages as fast as a court reporter. But this is just the fantasy of the uninitiated. I know some very great writers, writers you love who write beautifully and have made a great deal of money, and not one of them sits down routinely feeling wildly enthusiastic and confident. Not one of them writes elegant first drafts. All right, one of them does, but we do not like her very much. We do not think that she has a rich inner life or that God likes her or can even stand her. (Although when I mentioned this to my priest friend Tom, he said you can safely assume you've created God in your own image when it turns out that God hates all the same people you do.)

Very few writers really know what they are doing until they've done it. Nor do they go about their business feeling dewy and thrilled. They do not type a few stiff warm-up sentences and then find themselves bounding along like huskies across the snow. One writer I know tells me that he sits down every morning and says to himself nicely, "It's not like you don't have a choice, because you do—you can either type, or kill yourself." We all often feel like we are pulling teeth, even those writers whose prose ends up being the most natural and fluid. The right words and sentences just do not come pouring out like ticker tape most of the time. Now, Muriel Spark is said to have felt that she was taking dictation from God every morning—sitting there, one supposes, plugged into a Dictaphone, typing away, humming. But this is a very hostile and aggressive position. One might hope for bad things to rain down on a person like this.

For me and most of the other writers I know, writing is not rapturous. In fact, the only way I can get anything written at all is to write really, really shitty first drafts.

The first draft is the child's draft, where you let it all pour out and then let it romp all over the place, knowing that no one is going to see it and that you can shape it later. You just let this childlike part of you channel whatever voices and visions come through and onto the page. If one of the characters wants to say, "Well, so what, Mr. Poopy Pants?," you let her. No one is going to see it. If the kid wants to get into really sentimental, weepy, emotional territory, you let him. Just get it all down on paper because there may be something great in those six crazy pages that you would never have gotten to by more rational, grown-up means. There may be something in the very last line of the very last paragraph on page six that you just love, that is so beautiful or wild that you now know what you're supposed to be writing about, more or less, or in what direction you might go—but there was no way to get to this without first getting through the first five and a half pages.

I used to write food reviews for California magazine before it folded. (My writing food reviews had nothing to do with the magazine folding, although every single review did cause a couple of canceled subscriptions. Some readers took umbrage at my comparing mounds of vegetable puree with various ex-presidents' brains.) These reviews always took two days to write. First I'd go to a restaurant several times with a few opinionated, articulate friends in tow. I'd sit there writing down everything anyone said that was at all interesting or funny. Then on the following Monday I'd sit down at my desk with my notes and try to write the review. Even after I'd been doing this for years, panic would set in. I'd try to write a lead, but instead I'd write a couple of dreadful sentences, XX them out, try again, XX everything out, and then feel despair and worry settle on my chest like an x-ray apron. It's over, I'd think calmly. I'm not going to be able to get the magic to work this time. I'm ruined. I'm through. I'm toast. Maybe, I'd think, I can get my old job back as a clerk-typist. But probably not. I'd get up and study my teeth in the mirror for a while. Then I'd stop, remember to breathe, make a few phone calls, hit the kitchen and chow down. Eventually I'd go back and sit down at my desk, and sigh for the next ten minutes. Finally I would pick up my one-inch picture frame, stare into it as if for the answer, and every time the answer would come: all I had to do was to write a really shitty first draft of, say, the opening paragraph. And no one was going to see it.

So I'd start writing without reining myself in. It was almost just typing, just making my fingers move. And the writing would be terrible. I'd write a lead paragraph that was a whole page, even though the entire review could only be three pages long, and then I'd start writing up descriptions of the food, one dish at a time, bird by bird, and the critics would be sitting on my shoulders, commenting like cartoon characters. They'd be pretending to snore, or rolling their eyes at my overwrought descriptions, no matter how hard I tried to tone those descriptions down, no matter how conscious I was of what a friend said to me gently in my early days of restaurant reviewing. "Annie," she said, "it is just a piece of chicken. It is just a bit of cake."

But because by then I had been writing for so long, I would eventually let myself trust the process—sort of, more or less. I'd write a first draft that was maybe twice as long as it should be, with a self-indulgent and boring beginning, stupefying descriptions of the meal, lots of quotes from my black-humored friends that made them sound more like the Manson girls than food lovers, and no ending to speak of. The whole thing would be so long and incoherent and hideous that for the rest of the day I'd obsess about getting creamed by a car before I could write a decent second draft. I'd worry that people would read what I'd written and believe that the accident had really been a suicide, that I had panicked because my talent was waning and my mind was shot.

The next day, I'd sit down, go through it all with a colored pen, take out everything I possibly could, find a new lead somewhere on the second page, figure out a kicky place to end it, and then write a second draft. It always turned out fine, sometimes even funny and weird and helpful. I'd go over it one more time and mail it in.

Then, a month later, when it was time for another review, the whole process would start again, complete with the fears that people would find my first draft before I could rewrite it.

Almost all good writing begins with terrible first efforts. You need to start somewhere. Start by getting something—anything—down on paper. A friend of mine says that the first draft is the down draft—you just get it down. The second draft is the up draft—you fix it up. You try to say what you have to say more accurately. And the third draft is the dental draft, where you check every tooth, to see if it's loose or cramped or decayed, or even, God help us, healthy.

The Principles of Poor Writing

Paul W. Merrill

Books and articles on good writing are numerous, but where can you find sound, practical advice on how to write poorly? Poor writing is so common that every educated person ought to know something about it. Many scientists actually do write poorly, but they probably perform by ear without perceiving clearly how their results are achieved. An article on the principles of poor writing might help. The author considers himself well qualified to prepare such an article; he can write poorly without half trying.

The average student finds it surprisingly easy to acquire the usual tricks of poor writing. To do a consistently poor job, however, one must grasp a few essential principles:

I. Ignore the reader.
II. Be verbose, vague, and pompous.
III. Do not revise.

IGNORE THE READER

The world is divided into two great camps: yourself and others. A little obscurity or indirection in writing will keep the others at a safe distance; if they get close, they may see too much.

Write as if for a diary. Keep your mind on a direct course between yourself and the subject; don't think of the reader—he makes a bad triangle. This is

From Paul W. Merrill, "The Principles of Poor Writing" *The Scientific Monthly*, Vol. 64, No. 1 (Jan., 1947), pp. 72–74. Reprinted with permission from AAAS.

fundamental. Constant and alert consideration of the probable reaction of the reader is a serious menace to poor writing; moreover, it requires mental effort. A logical argument is that if you write poorly enough, your readers will be too few to merit any attention whatever.

Ignore the reader wherever possible. If the proposed title, for example, means something to you, stop right there; think no further. If the title baffles or misleads the reader, you have won the first round. Similarly, all the way through you must write for yourself, not for the reader. Practice a deadpan technique, keeping your facts and ideas all on the same level of emphasis with no telltale hints of relative importance or logical sequence. Use long sentences containing many ideas loosely strung together. *And* is the connective most frequently employed in poor writing because it does not indicate cause and effect, nor does it distinguish major ideas from subordinate ones. *Because* seldom appears in poor writing, nor does the semicolon—both are replaced by *and*.

Camouflage transitions in thought. Avoid such connectives as *moreover, nevertheless, on the other hand.* If unable to resist the temptation to give some signal for a change in thought, use *however.* A poor sentence may well begin with *however* because to the reader, with no idea what comes next, *however* is too vague to be useful. A good sentence begins with the subject or with a phrase that needs emphasis.

The "hidden antecedent" is a common trick of poor writing. Use a pronoun to refer to a noun a long way back, or to one decidedly subordinate in thought or syntax; or the pronoun may refer to something not directly expressed. If you wish to play a little game with the reader, offer him the wrong antecedent as bait; you may be astonished how easy it is to catch the poor fish.

In ignoring the reader avoid parallel constructions which give the thought away too easily. I need not elaborate, for you probably employ inversion frequently. It must have been a naive soul who said, "When the thought is parallel, let the phrases be parallel."

In every technical paper omit a few items that most readers need to know. You had to discover these things the hard way; why make it easy for the reader? Avoid defining symbols; never specify the units in which data are presented. Of course it will be beneath your dignity to give numerical values of constants in formulae. With these omissions, some papers may be too short; lengthen them by explaining things that do not need explaining. In describing tables, give special attention to self-explanatory headings; let the reader hunt for the meaning of $P^1 r_0$.

BE VERBOSE, VAGUE, AND POMPOUS

The cardinal sin of poor writing is to be concise and simple. Avoid being specific; it ties you down. Use plenty of deadwood: include many superfluous words and phrases. Wishful thinking suggests to a writer that verbosity somehow serves as a cloak or even as a mystic halo by which an idea may be glorified. A cloud of words may conceal defects in observation or analysis, either by opacity or by diverting the reader's attention. Introduce abstract nouns at the drop of a hat—even in those *cases* where the *magnitude* of the *motion* in a downward *direction* is inconsiderable. Make frequent use of the words *case, character, condition, former* and *latter, nature, suck, very.*

Poor writing, like good football, is strong on razzle-dazzle, weak on information. Adjectives are frequently used to bewilder the reader. It isn't much trouble to make them gaudy or hyperbolic; at least they can be flowery and inexact.

DEADWOOD

Bible: Render to Caesar the things that are Caesar's.
Poor: In the case of Caesar it might well be considered appropriate from a moral or ethical point of view to render to that potentate all of those goods and materials of whatever character or quality which can be shown to have had their original source in any portion of the domain of the latter.

Shakespeare: I am no orator as Brutus is.
Poor: The speaker is not what might be termed as adept in the profession of public speaking, as might be properly stated of Mr. Brutus. (Example from P. W. Swain. *Amer. J. Physics,* 13, 318, 1945.)

Concise: The dates of several observations are in doubt.
Poor: It should be mentioned that in the case of several observations there is room for considerable doubt concerning the correctness of the dates on which they were made.

Reasonable: Exceptionally rapid changes occur in the spectrum.
Poor: There occur in the spectrum changes which are quite exceptional in respect to the rapidity of their advent.

Reasonable: Formidable difficulties, both mathematical and observational, stand in the way.
Poor: There are formidable difficulties of both a mathematical and an observational nature that stand in the way.

CASE

Reasonable: Two sunspots changed rapidly.
Poor: There are two cases where sunspots changed with considerable rapidity.

Reasonable: Three stars are red.
Poor: In three cases the stars are red in color.

RAZZLE-DAZZLE

Immaculate precision of observation and extremely delicate calculations.
. . .

It would prove at once a world imponderable, etherealized. Our actions would grow grandific.

Well for us that the pulsing energy of the great life-giving dynamo in the sky never ceases. Well, too, that we are at a safe distance from the flame-licked whirlpools into which our earth might drop like a pellet of waste fluff shaken into the live coals of a grate fire.

DO NOT REVISE

Write hurriedly, preferably when tired. Have no plan; write down items as they occur to you. The article will thus be spontaneous and poor. Hand in your manuscript the moment it is finished. Rereading a few days later might lead to revision—which seldom, if ever, makes the writing worse. If you submit your manuscript to colleagues (a bad practice), pay no attention to their criticisms or comments. Later resist firmly any editorial suggestions. Be strong and infallible; don't let anyone break down your personality. The critic may be trying to help you or he may have an ulterior motive, but the chance of his causing improvement in your writing is so great that you must be on guard.

Final suggestion for poor writing
Do not read:

Allbutt, Clifford. *Notes on the Composition of Scientific Papers.* Macmillan, 1923.

Flesch, Rudolf. *The Art of Plain Talk.* Harper, 1946.

Graves and Hodge. *The Reader Over Your Shoulder.* Macmillan, 1943.

Quiller-Couch, Arthur. *On the Art of Writing.* [V]. Putnam, 1928.

Suggestions to Authors of Papers Submitted for Publication by the United States Geological Survey. U. S. Gov. Ptg. Off., 1935.

Five Principles for Getting Good Ideas

Jack Rawlins

Brains that get good ideas follow five principles:

> Don't begin with a topic.
> Think all the time.
> To get something out, put something in.
> Go from little, concrete things to big, abstract things.
> Connect.

We'll talk about each in turn.

DON'T BEGIN WITH A TOPIC

Essays rarely begin with subject matter alone. Why would a person say out of the blue, "I think I'll write about linoleum, or the national debt"? Nor are the kernels of essays always "good ideas"—they often aren't *ideas* at all, in the sense of whole assertions. Thinking begins in lots of ways:

> *With a question:* "Is there any real difference between the Republicans and the Democrats anymore?" "Why is Ralph so mad at me?"
>
> *With a problem:* "I'm always behind in my work." "Violet crimes against women are on the increase."

With a purpose: "I want to tell people about what's really going on in this class." "I want to let people know about alternatives to traditional medicine."

With a thesis: "There are cheaper, healthier alternatives to regular grocery stores." "Old people are the victims of silent injustice in our culture."

With a feeling: anger, frustration, surprise.

With a sensation or image: a smell, a glimpse of a bird in flight, an eye-catching TV ad.

What shall we call that thing an essay begins with—the seed, the spark, the inspiration, the sense of "gotcha"? I'll call it a prompt.

THINK ALL THE TIME

If you have a sense of humor, you know that the surest way to prevent yourself from being funny is to have someone (even yourself) demand that you be funny *now*. Comedians have always bemoaned the fact that people introduce them to friends by saying, "This is Milton. He's a riot. Be funny, Milton." Thinking's the same way. Being put on the spot is the surest way of preventing the creative juices from flowing.

So don't expect to discover a good prompt by sitting down for a scheduled half-hour of profundity. Minds that think well think all the time. One prolific student wrote that she goes through the world "looking for *writable* things" and is thought weird by her friends because she scribbles notes to herself at parties.

Thinking all the time sounds like work, but it isn't. Your mind works all the time whether you want it to or not, the same way your body moves all the times. Any yogi will tell you that it takes years of practice to learn to turn the mind *off*, even for a minute or two. And it's physiologically impossible for your brain to get tired, which is why you can study or write all day, go to bed, and find your mind still racing while your body cries for rest. So I'm really not asking your brain to do anything new; I'm just asking you to *listen* to it.

TO GET SOMETHING OUT, PUT SOMETHING IN

One popular, poisonous image for thinking is the light bulb flashing on over someone's head—the notion that ideas spring from within us, caused by nothing. To become good thinkers, we have to replace that image with another; think of ideas as billiard balls set in motion when something collides with them. Ideas are *re*actions—we have them in response to other things.

A thinker thinks as life passes through him and does what I call "talking back to the world." Many of us separate our input and output modes; we are either putting information into our brains or asking our brains to produce thoughts, but we don't do both at the same time. I call such people data sponges. But the best time to try to get things out is when things are going in. Let them bounce off you and strike sparks. People do this naturally until they've been taught to be passive; try reading a book to a three-year-old, and listen to her react to everything she hears and sees, or take her to a movie and watch her struggle not to talk back to the screen.

Are you a data sponge? To find out, answer the following questions.

> Do you find yourself mentally talking back to the newspaper when you read it?
>
> Do you write in the margins of books you read?
>
> Are at least 25 percent of the notes you take during course reading or lectures your own thoughts, questions, doubts, and reactions?
>
> As you meet up with life's outrages, do you find yourself complaining to imaginary audiences?
>
> After a movie, do you feel like you're going to burst until you find someone to talk about it?
>
> When you listen to a speaker or a teacher, do you find yourself itching to get to the question-and-answer period?

If you said yes to these questions, you're not a sponge. If you said no, you're going to have to practice your reacting skills.

GO FROM LITTLE, CONCRETE THINGS TO BIG, ABSTRACT THINGS

This principle is a logical consequence of the one before. Since ideas come best in reaction to life's incoming billiard balls, the best thinking follows a predictable course: from little, concrete bits of experience to large abstract implications. You see an ad on TV and start thinking about it, and it leads you to speculations on American consumerism, media manipulation, and the marketing of women's bodies. You overhear a snippet of conversation between a parent and child at the grocery store and start thinking about it, and it leads you to speculations on American child-rearing practices, the powerlessness of children, parental brainwashing, and antiyouth bigotry.

Here's what going from little particulars to big issues is like. I was sitting doing nothing one day when my eyes fell on a box of Girl Scout cookies. The box had on it a picture of a girl and the slogan, "I'm not like anyone else." I reacted. I thought, "Gosh, that sounds lonely." And I valued the reaction enough to notice it and think about it. It led me to a big issue: How does Americans' love of individuality affect their ability to be members of a culture? And I formulated a thesis: Americans love their individuality so much that they'll cut themselves off from everything and everyone to get it. Being unlike everyone else is a curse, because it means you're separated from other *human beings by your differentness*. I was raised a proud individualist, and I've only recently realized that the reward for being unique is loneliness.

I went from little things to big issues when I drew essays out of one writer's life. When she mentioned that she couldn't drink too heavily in high school because it would affect her shot-putting, I instantly saw the abstract issue illustrated by her experience: People who have things they love dare not practice self-destructive behavior, because they'll destroy what they love in the process. So alcoholism or drug abuse is neither a crime nor a disease nor a moral failure in the individual; it's a symptom of a social failure, the failure of our society to offer the alcoholic or drug addict a life too precious to risk destroying.

Beginning writers want to start with large abstractions, in the mistaken belief that the bigger the optic is, the more there is to say about it. It doesn't work out that way. Usually the first sentence of the essay tells whether the writer knows this or not. Essays on friendship that begin "Friendship is one of the most important things in life" are doomed, because the writer doesn't know it. Essays that begin "Mary was my best friend in high school" will thrive, because the writer does know it.

CONNECT

Those who think well make connections between things. An essay begins when two previously unrelated bits in the brain meet and discover a connection. Usually a new stimulus hitches up with an old bit stored long ago in the memory; the incoming billiard ball hits an old one that's just lying there, and they fly off together.

It's hard to learn the connecting skill if you don't have it already. Here's what it feels like inside. One day I was sitting in an English Department faculty meeting, and we were discussing an administrative change. A colleague said, "We couldn't do that until we were sure our people would be protected." I thought momentarily, "I wonder how he knows who 'his people' are?" Months later I was vacationing in a small mountain town and picked up the local newspaper. On the front page was an article about the firing of a group of non-union construction workers. The boss had asked the union for workers, but none were available, so he trained out-of-work mill workers. Later the union rep showed up, announced that union workers were now available, and insisted that the others be fired. Something clicked, and I had an essay. My colleague's attitude and the union rep's were the same: I'll watch out for "my people," and everyone else can watch out for himself. I wanted to talk about why people think that way and how they learn to rise above it.

How did I make that connection? Incredible as it sounds, and unbeknownst to me, I must have been checking everything that came into my brain against the faculty-meeting remarks for a possible connection. Or perhaps I had opened a file in my mind labeled "people who think in terms of those who belong and those who don't" and dumped anything related in there as it came along.

I just read a great essay by Arthur Miller connecting the current prayer-in-school political debate with his memories of saying the Pledge of Allegiance in elementary school. What brought the two things together? Miller must have checked prayer in schools against everything in his memory relating to state-mandated loyalty and come up with recollections of third grade. That sounds exhausting, but we all know that when something clicks in memory, we haven't "worked" at all—in fact, the way to bring the connection that's on the tip of the tongue to the surface is to forget about it and let the subconscious do its work unwatched.

The more unlike two things are and the less obvious the connection between them is, the fresher and more stimulating the connection is when you make it. Finding a connection between mountain climbers and skydivers is merely okay; finding a connection between inflation rates and the incidence of breast cancer will make the world open its eyes. This is the Head Principle. Mr. Head was an aviation engineer who got interested in downhill skiing. Apparently no one had ever connected aircraft technology and skiing before; Mr. Head took a few runs down the hill and realized that he could make a better ski if he simply made it according to the principles and with the materials used in making airplane wings. He invented the Head ski, the first metal ski, and made millions of dollars. He then did the same thing in tennis, by inventing the Prince racket. Apparently aircraft engineers didn't play tennis either.

The Head Principle says you can't predict what will connect with what. So you can't tell yourself what information to seek. You can only take in experience and information voraciously and stir it all up together. If I had been formally researching stupid faculty remarks, I'd never have thought to read up on northern Californian construction workers. If you're writing about Charles Dickens and you read only about Charles Dickens, you're just guaranteeing you won't make any connections except those other Dickens scholars have already made. Instead, go read *Psychology Today*, read Nixon's memoirs, see a movie, watch a documentary on insect societies, or visit a mortuary. As you talk back to all of it, keep asking yourself, "What is this like? When have I thought things like this before? When was the last time I reacted like this?" When I read about the construction workers, I reacted, and I remembered that I'd had a conversation with myself like that one before sometime. Perhaps that's the key to connecting.

It's easy to block ideas from coming by practicing the exact opposite of our idea-getting principles. Just set aside a time for idea-getting, cut yourself off from the outside world by locking yourself in a stimulus-free study room, and muse on a cosmic abstraction. If you're doing any of that, your idea-getting regime needs overhauling.

Unlearn to Write

Donald M. Murray

Those mornings when I sit at my desk and no words come, when the draft staggers and stumbles to a halt, or I read what I have written with shame and disgust and punch "Delete," I often find I have been following the rules drilled into my skull by Miss Leavitt, the high school teacher I had in the eleventh and twelfth grade.

They were the rules I had first been taught in elementary school, retaught in junior high school, and the first two years in high school. They were absolute, unquestioned, always followed by the writers we studied. When I wrote outside of class, I often broke the rules or simply ignored them, but they sounded so certain, so logical, so authoritative—pun intended—that years later, like a forest fire that travels underground and suddenly bursts out unexpectedly, I find I am following one or more of them. I have to stop and once more unlearn the rules guaranteed to produce ineffective and graceless writing.

My teachers were well intentioned but they were readers who did not write themselves.

Later in this chapter you will be introduced to a process that published writers use to write and that you will be able to adjust to your way of thinking, your experience with writing, and to the writing task itself. But first you—and I—have to unlearn to write.

It might be fun for you to stop right now and write down the absolute rules you have been taught about writing to see if they match what I was taught and had to unlearn.

WHAT I HAD TO UNLEARN

1. Know What You Want to Say Before You Say It

When I wrote in school, the teacher would march up and down the aisles repeating, "Know what you want to say before you say it." Most of the time she would require that we write a thesis statement at the top of the page, telling what the writing we hadn't yet done would say.

Writers are writers, however, because the act of writing is a voyage into the unknown; it's an adventure in discovering what you know, but didn't know you knew; in connecting in ways you haven't connected what you know before; in discovering what you need to know.

Once in a while I do not know what I am going to say or have an assignment that limits discovery. In those cases I have to *unknow* to find my own way to the predicted meaning. The best writing is traitor to intent. It grows, line by line, from a terrifying emptiness, when there is no purpose, no topic, no clear meaning.

Writers write and discover what they have to say as drafts. It is the writing not the writer that speaks. Novelist and short story writer Donald Barthelme explains:

Writing is a process of dealing with not-knowing, a forcing of what and how.

> We have all heard novelists testify to the fact that, beginning a new book, they are utterly baffled as to how to proceed, what should be written and how it might be written, even though they've done a dozen. At best there's a slender intuition, not much greater than an itch. Art is not difficult because it wishes to be difficult, rather because it wishes to be art. However much the writer might long to be, in his work, simple, honest, straightforward, these virtues are no longer available to him. He discovers that in being simple, honest, straightforward, nothing much happens: he speaks the speakable, whereas we are looking for the as-yet unspeakable, the as-yet unspoken.

People ask, "Where do you get your ideas?" I answer, "I don't have ideas." I am terrified of ideas. I may have a shard of ancient Indian pottery, a fragment of bone that may be dog or dinosaur, a burr under the saddle, an answer that has not yet met its question, a contradiction to a certain belief, a fragment of language that contains a tension, a hint that there is as-yet unseen world around the next turn in the road that I must explore. As Graham Greene said, "The novel is an unknown man and I have to find him."

When I am lucky, I don't even have that. I have a panic nothingness and I start to describe something that I caught in the corner of my eye, not knowing I saw it, and as I write the barely remembered scene becomes clearer—draft by draft—the way blank photographic paper slowly reveals its image in a tray of developer.

I have the world—memory and vision—and words. That is enough. I write and what I find myself saying reveals what I have to say.

2. Form Comes Before Content

My teacher would assign the form—a literary essay, a personal essay, an argument before the topic. Now I know the form should grow organically as the writer writes to discover what to say and how to say it. The blueprint for an argument may come from a textbook as a blueprint for a bridge comes from a textbook on building bridges, but it must be adapted to the width of the river, the current, the makeup of the banks and the river bottom, the traffic it will bear. The form of the argument should grow according to the facts on both sides, the proponent and opposition, the place the case is being argued and the audience. The argument evolves as the writer gathers the facts and anticipates the reader's doubts and questions.

Writers should not build a form and then pour concrete into it, but write and then see what develops. In school we build walls between fiction and nonfiction, narrative and exposition, poetry and argument, but the writer breaks down those walls using dialogue and scene in nonfiction, argument and logic in fiction.

3. Correct Spelling, Grammar, Mechanics Are Essential in the First Draft

Ernest Hemingway said, "Prose is architecture not interior decoration." It is important for the accurate communication of meaning to follow the traditions of language on the final draft. They are the conventions reader and writer share. Most of the time, in fact, we will follow these conventions, but if we concentrate on them while writing, our language becomes stiff and meaningless.

I am a terrible speller. I use a bad speller's dictionary, a word list book, my computer spell check, and my wife to correct my spelling before I submit a draft to an editor, but if I stop to spell well as I write, I may lose the river of thought that is carrying me towards meaning.

The same is true of grammar and punctuation. In fact, if I am writing what I have not written before, my language often becomes awkward as I struggle to find what I want to say and then how to make it clear to me and then my reader. In fact, the breakthrough into a new meaning often comes when the syntax collapses and I find myself saying badly what I will later make clear.

4. Long Is Better Than Short

My teachers had good reason to teach us vocabulary through the grades, introducing us to longer and more complex words. They had to help us escape the limitation of brief subject-verb-object sentences, introducing clauses and complex sentence structures. The same thing was true of paragraphs and beyond. The unintended message was that longer is better and, in fact, those students who used big multisyllabic words, long mountain trails of sentences, huge overpacked paragraphs, page upon page saying what could have been said in a few words were rewarded with praise and As.

When these students, partly because they have gotten such good grades, try to become writers, they discover that short is better than long. Writers use the shortest words, shortest sentences, and shortest paragraphs they can. Since the ideas they have to communicate are often complicated, the shortest words that contain the appropriate meaning may be long ones and the shortest sentences may be full of clauses.

5. Don't Write as You Speak

I was taught NOT to write as I spoke. I was instructed to follow the writing style of the previous century and write in a formal manner. Speech and writing were taught to me as separate subjects by different teachers. We live, however, in an informal, dress-down age. We appreciate writing that gives the illusion of speech, good writing as conversation. Of course it isn't realistic—uh—it isn't like—you know—uh—what I sorta, you know—uh—mean.

Graceful and effective writing today sounds like idealized speech, flowing naturally toward meaning. Readers want to hear the individual voice of the writer, the writer's way of speaking tuned to the meaning of what is being said and the audience to which it is aimed.

I write aloud as most writers do, hearing what I am writing before I see it. I can write with the screen turned off. Try it yourself. You should be able to write as well or better than when it is turned on.

6. Always Outline First

Not always. You can't draw a map of a country you have never visited. If you are using writing to explore a new territory, you probably can't write an outline until after the first draft, when it may be very helpful.

It depends, of course, on the form you are writing as well as your familiarity with the subject. In writing this edition of *Write to Learn,* my editor and I had to agree on an outline. But even then the outline is not the rigid plan I was taught in high school, but a sketch. Later, I will introduce ways to outline, but it does not have to come before the first draft.

7. The First Draft Should Be the Last Draft

Sometimes that does happen. I have been writing a weekly newspaper column for sixteen years. I know the form, the length, the audience, my persona, and voice. Most of the time I revise and edit as I go along and when I finish, but last week the editor—who was right—demanded three major revisions. For years when I wrote magazine articles I wrote three drafts of each one and revised each draft ten times. I went through the article thirty times.

Most of the time I have to write a *discovery draft* to find out what I have to say, a *development draft* to fill out and document what I have discovered, and a *clarifying draft* to make it clear to myself and the reader.

In school, I was only required to rewrite when I wrote a bad paper. If I was singled out to rewrite it was because the teacher felt I had failed. The same was true when I started working on a newspaper, but when I graduated to magazines and books, the first thing I had to learn was to rewrite. Not just because my first drafts failed—and they did—but because it took many drafts to discover and communicate my subject. For writers, writing is rewriting and I learned to enjoy the craft of cutting, adding, and moving around so the subject became clear to me and, eventually, to my readers.

8. There Is One Right Way

I believed longer than I like to admit what my teacher seemed to believe: There is one right way. If I could find the one right word, the single right sentence, the only right paragraph, I would become a writer. What I have learned as a writer is that there are many wrong ways and many right ways. The way of the writer is selection and choice; the method, trial and error. Writing is an experimental science.

There are no rights and wrongs in writing. You can be absolutely correct and write badly, or you can write well, but not be correct according to the "rules."

The writer confronts—word by word, line by line, paragraph by paragraph—the demanding question: Does it work? Does it advance the meaning? Does it fit within the context? Is it accurate? Is it graceful? Is it clear? These questions are principles of effective writing. They must be asked draft after draft.

James Thurber commanded, "Don't get it right, get it written."

When I fail, I go right back to first grade. Miss Kelly jams me in the waste-basket, my feet sticking out by my head like rabbit ears. I am humiliated. I despair. I want to quit but I have to remind myself that failure is essential. If

I am not failing, I am not writing. I am repeating what I have said before—in the way I have said it before.

The wrong word leads to the right word, the broken syntax points toward the phrase that clarifies. Writing is not stenography. Writing is thinking, a process of trial-and-error experimentation in which failure reveals what we cannot yet say, but where the saying may lay hidden. Novelist Jon Fowles tells us, "Follow the accident, fear the fixed plan—that is the rule."

9. Revision and Editing Are the Same

In school I was told that when I finished a draft, I was to check the spelling, grammatical usage, and punctuation. Correctness was all.

As a writer I learned that writing was a search for a significant meaning and then communicating it. Correctness was the last part of the writing process, patting your hair in place, straightening your tie.

Revision is literally the process of re-seeing. When writers revise they reconsider the subject, the genre, the focus, its development, its voice. Writers revise first to discover and develop what they have to say and then to shape it so readers who have no interest in reading the message will read it.

Editing is the process of clarification. Writers go through the entire piece line by line, again and again, to make sure each detail is accurate, that every word or phrase that needs to be defined is, to cut what is unnecessary, to add what is necessary, to move words around to make the meaning clear, and to follow the conventions of language if they help the reader receive and understand the meaning.

10. Say What You Are Going to Say, Say It, Say What You've Said

I can hear my teacher repeating this counsel again and again and again. She demanded an introduction, a repetitive body of prose, and a conclusion. It was once good advice, and in fact such an organization may be required in certain situations, in writing scientific papers, for example. But the general reader today does not have the patience to read the same thing three times.

In this book we will demonstrate the lede, or lead, that propels the reader right into the subject in the first paragraph, in the first sentences, in the first words. And the book will also show the conclusion that implies the meaning without insulting readers by telling them what to think or how to feel.

11. Write in Generalities for a General Audience

Makes sense, but it doesn't work. Universal writing rises from the specific, the resonating detail that sparks emotions, memories, thoughts in the mind of the reader. As novelist and essayist James Carroll says:

The law of particularity forces fiction writers, poets, and dramatists to obsess over details, instances, and concrete images, while treating the experience of one or two characters as if it matters as much as the sum total experience of the entire human race. To writers, a moment in time, properly rendered, is worth all time—a single, vividly imagined place is worth the cosmos.

The more particular I am—writing of my Scots Baptist grandmother, for example—the more readers read the memories of their Russian Jewish, Irish Catholic, Chinese Buddhist grandmothers. Accurate, resonating specifics makes readers read—and trust what they read.

12. Talent Is Rare

Talent is common. I once wrote with a class of elementary students so talented I asked them how they were chosen. They had IQs between 80 and 85—and a teacher who respected the stories they had to tell and their potential to tell them. Every class I taught had students that were more talented than I was. I did not have a freshman English class that had a student who could not become a professional—if they worked at it. I have had students who have careers in writing and editing with verbal scores in the 300s on their SATs.

What most of my students did NOT have was the desire to be published and the work habits to make it possible. The distinguished short story writer Andre Dubus declares, "Talent is cheap. What matters is discipline." Novelist E. M. Forster testifies, "The act of writing inspires me," and Graham Greene says, "I have no talent. It's just a question of working, of being willing to put in the time. . . . If one wants to write, one simply has to organize one's life in a mass of little habits."

13. Easy Writing Is Bad Writing

Writing should be easy. The cliché states, "easy writing makes hard reading." Just the opposite. Hard, constipated writing makes difficult reading, writing that is not read. We make writing hard out of displaced virtue.

I work hard to make writing easy, remembering the times when the writing went well and repeating those attitude and conditions.

14. Study What Is Published and Imitate It

Wrong. It is logical, but what is being published can be reproduced by staff members or experienced freelancers. Editors are looking for the voices they haven't yet heard telling the stories they don't know exist in ways they have not yet imagined. As Doris Lessing says, "You have to remember that nobody ever wants a new writer. You have to create your own demand."

How do you do that? By respecting your own vision of the world. Sandra Cisneros says it best:

> Imagine yourself at your kitchen table, in your pajamas. Imagine one person you'd allow to see you that way, and write in the voice you'd use to that friend. Write about what makes you different.

I have found that all the things that made me strange—even frightening—to my family, my neighbors, my pastor and my church members, my teachers and schoolmates, and continue to puzzle my wife and my children, colleagues and friends, and even myself are those things that I have to offer the world.

As my writer friend Chip Scanlan says: "Do the writing only you can do."

15. Don't Make Mistakes

Failure is essential to the writer. It is the failures that reveal the possibilities for good writing. We have to write badly to write well. Writers take risks, they take chances.

Be promiscuous—as a writer. Write in as many forms and voices for as many readers or publications as possible. Write what you know and what you need to know and what you will know only by writing. As Annie Dillar advises,

> One of the few things I know about writing is this: spend it all, shoot it, play it, lose it, all, right away, every time. Do not hoard what seems good for a later place in the book, or for another book; give it, give it all, give it now. The impulse to save something good for a better place later is the signal to spend it now. Something more will arise for later, something better. These things fill from behind, like well water.

John Jerome says, "Perfect is the enemy of good."

16. You Can't Teach Writing

Of course you can. My students taught themselves to write better in my classes than they wrote before the class. Take instruction from the writer Ursula Le Guin:

> If you want to be a tuba player you get a tuba, and some tuba music. And you ask the neighbors to move away or put cotton in their ears. And you probably get a tuba teacher, because there are a lot of objective rules and techniques to both written music and to tuba performance. And then you sit down and you play the tuba, every day, every week, every month, year after year, until you are good at playing tuba; until you can—if you desire—play the truth on the tuba.

It is exactly the same with writing. You sit down, and you do it, and you do it, and you do it, until you have learned how to do it.

PART 5

Student Essays

Behuniak 1

An Education With Anxiety

Kaylie Behuniak

First Grade

One two three four fi---- that girl took my marshmallow.

I asked her why she did it, she said she dropped one of hers. I told her that she shouldn't steal my marshmallows just because she dropped hers, she said watch me and stuffed the rest of my marshmallows in her mouth.

I felt my eyes flood with tears and I wanted to cry, but I didn't want to be called a baby. I felt my fists clench and the desire to punch her pretty little nose right off her face, but I didn't want to get sent to the principal's office. I felt my nostrils flare as I reached across the table to grab her remaining marshmallows, but a voice stopped me.

Kaylie what do you think you're doing? Just because you ate your marshmallows doesn't give you the right to steal someone else's. I want you to apologize to Jenna, and then go to the 'take a break corner.' I was dumbfounded. I never got in trouble. I was a good girl. How could the teacher think I would steal Jenna's marshmallows? Jenna stole mine!

As I shamefully made my way to the timeout corner disguised with stress balls and a notebook as the 'take a break' corner, I saw the smirk on Jenna's face and the disappointment on my teacher's. I wanted to say something, I really did, but I knew there was no point. While I was mad at Jenna, I was more scared of what my teacher thought of me. I panicked as I thought about my teacher never speaking to me again or making me repeat first grade. I had been caught red-handed trying to take marshmallows that weren't my own.

I didn't have the upper hand, and little did I know that I was going to spend the rest of my life fighting for it.

Second Grade

Maybe if she hadn't told me, I wouldn't be afraid. Maybe if she hadn't told me, I wouldn't be different. But then again if she hadn't told me, I wouldn't be who I am or where I am today.

We were out on the playground and one of my friends ran over to me. I asked her why she wasn't in school yesterday, and I told her about all the activities she missed: tracking the butterflies we were hatching, doing a new subtraction mad minute, and playing bean bag sneaker tag in gym class. She told me she had the stomach bug and that her mom made her stay home because she had diarrhea. I shrugged it off and we went back to running around, like every other 7-year-old on the playground.

That night I was playing with my dollhouse in the basement when I felt it, I felt the pain in my stomach and the urge to go to the bathroom. I ran upstairs to the bathroom and yelled for my mother.

That night a gear in my brain shifted ever so slightly out of place. That night my brain made the unfortunate connection of someone I know having the stomach bug, to me getting the stomach bug. That night was the beginning of my decade long battle of sleepless nights, panic attacks, and irrational worries.

Every night when I closed my eyes to go to sleep, my mind would race from one irrational worry to the next until eventually the lights went dark and I crawled further into an endless tunnel of fear and panic.

Third Grade

I had just learned cursive, I had just learned multiplication, and I had just learned how to read actual chapter books. I compiled folders for each subject and filled them with practice problems and worksheets. I kept myself busy with my schoolwork; in the mornings when I got up, on the bus ride to school, before class started, at lunch, on the bus ride home from school, before dinner, after dinner, and before I went to bed, I wrote stories, read books, and solved math problems. I always kept a notebook by my side in case of the dreaded down time.

My teachers thought I was organized, my parents thought I was studious, and my friends thought I was prepared; I wasn't about to tell them that I was afraid. I never left any time for fear to swoop in and knock me off my feet.

I kept myself busy so that fear couldn't pull the rug out from under me as I tiptoed across it.

Fourth Grade

He kissed me on the bus ride back from the Eli Whitney Museum, and I brought him chocolate covered almonds, not knowing about his tree nut allergy. We were the Ken and Barbie of Room 48, and everybody knew it. He asked me to be his girlfriend, and I said why not? He was my first (and last) boyfriend and that made our classmates jealous.

Soon after we became "boyfriend and girlfriend," the rest of the class started pairing up. We felt betrayed, like all of the attention that was once on us had vanished. So he did what any 10-year-old boy would do in that situation: he asked me to marry him. When I said yes, all attention turned back to us.

When my "wedding day" finally arrived and the recess bell rang, I saw my classmates standing by the pine tree alter. I heard Patrick Munn humming a poorly tuned rendition of the wedding march. I could smell the freshly cut wood chips on the playground, but all I felt was fear.

It was a feeling I was used to, but getting used to fear is much different than managing it. So I did what I had learned to do best, I ran away.

Fifth Grade

My body couldn't take another sleepless night or another day full of paranoia, so I hit a wall. My body was so overcome with fear that I began shaking at the thought of going to school to be around a bunch of sick kids, so I left. I left my class, I left my friends, I left everything I knew to finally get help.

I remember the Friday night clearly. I had had another rough day, as usual, and I was exhausted from the lack of sleep I had been getting. I creeped down the stairs, stepping over the creaky fourth step, and walked into my mom's room. As soon as I crossed from the tile of the hallway to the carpet of my mom's room, I broke down.

I fell to the floor and cried more than I had ever cried in my life. I told her I couldn't take another sleepless night, or another panic attack, or another day of anxiety controlling my life. I finally told her that I needed help. She called my dad and the three of us drove to Hartford Children's Hospital, where I would begin my road to recovery.

Those two weeks in the hospital were the worst two weeks of my life, but they allowed me to get the help I knew I needed. For the first time in years, I saw an end to the tunnel I had been crawling through.

When I eventually returned to school my life was different. All of the classmates I once called my friends, looked at me like I was the walking Ebola virus. No 11-year-old wanted to be friends with the girl with the disability, and coming from the girl with the disability, that hurt.

Having left school early 123 days on top of the 28 days I flat out missed, I spent the last two months of the year trying to catch up academically with the rest of my classmates. I reviewed lessons upon lessons in a last ditch effort to avoid repeating fifth grade.

Up until this year, I never allowed myself to stop running so that fear could never catch me, but this year I learned that no matter how *far* and how *fast* you run, eventually you'll end up hitting a wall.

Sixth Grade

It was early September, the school year had just begun and for once I was excited. I was excited for a fresh start, for a new year. Apparently, no matter how much I wanted a new start, the rest of my class disagreed.

I was riding the bus to school just like I did every morning, but this morning was different. This morning Elliot Monroe sat right behind me and pulled on my ponytail.

Hey Bee-hoo-nee-yak whatcha working on? Still doing schoolwork? Why are you always working on schoolwork?

Behuniak 6

I was still so taken aback from my ponytail being pulled that I remained silent.

What are you a baby? You can't talk because you're a baby. Baby Bee-hoo-nee-yak, baby Bee-hoo-nee-yak, baby Bee-hoo-nee-yak. . . .

I listened to his chanting for the whole ride to school as the tears filled my eyes. I couldn't let him see me cry, that's what he wanted, and I couldn't let him win. So I held my gaze on the seat in front of me for the remaining 5 minutes, until I stepped off and ran to the bathroom with tears running down my face.

I walked into class that day with a feeling I thought I had overcome, but as it turns out you can't overcome a fear you haven't yet embraced.

Seventh Grade

I have never been good with change so naturally a new school with new classmates and new teachers was not exciting me. I began having mini panic attacks whenever I got lost, or whenever someone new tried to talk to me.

I didn't know who knew about my past and who didn't, so I walked around like everyone did. I was so afraid of being seen as different or disabled that I froze whenever kids I had never met tried to talk to me.

I quickly became a social pariah, not because of my reputation, but because I was letting the fear of my reputation control me.

Though you know what they say, sometimes you have to take a step backward before you can finally take a step forward.

Eighth Grade

I stopped getting lost, started testing the waters of friendship, and was finally feeling comfortable with my school, and with myself. I had finally found a routine. I walked the same dimly lit hallways on my way to class, I sat with the same people at lunch, and I attended the weekly Wednesday meeting of the garden club. I was socializing and I was happier than I had been in years, and I never wanted that to change.

I remember the cold October day as I was busy weeding the little garden in the courtyard with my friend Jessica. We were laughing and throwing weeds into an already full wheelbarrow, when the clouds rolled in.

Alright everybody, it looks like it's about to rain so we are going to end the meeting early. Kaylie and Jessica, can you take the last wheelbarrow of weeds out back to the woods?

Jessica and I were more than willing to push the wheelbarrow across the courtyard, through the world language hallway, and then up the hill to the wooded area. I was pushing the wheelbarrow and Jessica was keeping it from tipping over by stabilizing the front. As we crossed through the world language hallway the wheelbarrow started to tip to the left, to compensate I jerked it to the right, right into the perfectly white wall.

In that moment I felt more "normal" than I had felt in years. I felt like a stupid 14-year-old getting herself into stupid shenanigans with her best friend. By the time we cleaned up the majority of the dirt and concealed the fresh dent with a nearby trash can, the rain had started.

As we ran back to the school through the pouring rain, I felt like every last worry was being washed out of my body.

Ninth Grade

Change hit me again like a satchel of rocks to the chest. All of a sudden, I was no longer in the same familiar environment with the same familiar routine, I was in high school. Suddenly I was walking to class with guys who had full beards and girls with faces plastered with makeup. I felt overwhelmed by the array of new students, but I also felt excited.

I didn't feel the nerves I had felt 2 years prior, I didn't suffer panic attacks whenever someone new tried to talk to me, but instead I embraced the fear and pushed myself to be as "normal" as I could. It wasn't until December that I realized how overrated "normal" really was.

Jessica and I were sitting on the wooden fence outside of the school waiting for her mom to pick us up, just watching the groups of juniors and seniors walk to their cars.

I hope one day we can be just like them, with the groups of friends and fancy cars, I told Jessica pointing to a group of senior girls laughing as they got into a white BMW.

Why? I don't. Those girls are so shallow, all they think about are boys and clothes, why would you ever want to be them. Those are the girls that make fun of girls like you and me who don't give a damn about makeup or clothes, or fancy cars. I was taken aback by how strongly Jessica felt about the "normal" girls.

You don't want to live a normal life, like those girls? I asked her. *Normality is a myth,* she said.

That night when I went home and looked at myself in the mirror, I couldn't picture my face underneath layers of paint

and powder, nor could I picture myself behind the wheel of a fancy car.

All I could picture was myself dancing in the rain with a ponytail and a baggy tee shirt.

Tenth Grade

I finally had friends who appreciated me for me, abnormality and all. My social life was at an all time high, academically I was thriving, but most importantly I was feeling anxiety free and comfortable with myself. I had given up on being "normal" and embraced my quirkiness.

I was surprised how easy just being myself was. I didn't have to worry about trying to fit in, I didn't have to try act like other girls my age, I simply had to be me.

The school always throws a lame Halloween parade around the track on Halloween, and this year I decided to dress up. The whole reason I didn't dress up for the parade last year was because people told me that no one dresses up if they don't have to for a club or a sports team, unless they want to be stared at and harshly judged. This year was different, this year I was going to dress up and not care if I was stared at or judged, because being in the parade made me happy.

Sure enough when Halloween came around, I got some strange glances and dirty looks. The important thing was that it made me happy to dress up and pretend to be someone else for a day. So what if girls shot daggers at me through their eyes, I was happy being me.

Ironically, I walk the halls dressed up in a costume and pretending to be someone I'm not for *one* day of the year, and I face judgment from girls who do it on a daily basis.

Eleventh Grade

The sirens wailed as we sped down the road, only briefly slowing down for stop signs. I placed my hand on the seat belt release, ready for when the ambulance stopped moving so I could jump out.

Behuniak 10

As soon as we pulled into the driveway and I opened the steel double doors, time froze. I grabbed the medical bag and the AED and jumped out of the ambulance. I followed the EMT's with the stretcher into the house where I saw the man seizing on the floor in front of me. I set up a portable suction and I did something I never thought I would be able to do; I suctioned vomit out of his mouth.

I never once thought I ever had a future in medicine, because I never once thought I could handle being around vomit. That's the reason I decided to become an EMT: so that I could face my fear of vomit through exposure.

I surprised myself that day when I was able to suction vomit out of a seizing man's mouth without panicking.

Maybe it was the adrenaline, maybe it was the pressure to save a man from choking, or maybe, just maybe, I had stepped into new territory and overcame a fear.

Twelfth Grade

I shouldn't have been here in this stupid white gown with an equally stupid white cap, at least not yet. I saw the stage on the football field covered with miscellaneous flowers, I heard the band start to play what sounds like a death march, I could smell the freshly cut cigar in Drake Benson's front pocket as I walked behind him, and all I felt was fear.

I wanted to run away and never look back . . . with 347 graduates who was going to notice if one disappeared? My parents would have, my sister would have, my friends would have, so I stayed. I walked across the flower covered stage to receive my diploma and shook the hands of 10 different administrators who would have rather been at home watching TV, all so that my family would be proud, and so that I could say that I did it.

Behuniak 11

As the ceremony concluded and it came time for all 347 graduates to move their 2018 tassel from the right side of their cap to the left, my fingers froze. I ran my thumb and index finger over the cold metal 8 in 2018 and I imagined a 9.

My mind flashed back to the very same administrators that had just shook my hand, telling 11-year-old me that there was only a 10% chance I would get to graduate with the class of 2018. The metal 8 in-between my fingers started to make my eyes fill with tears, but the abundance of caps being thrown into the air brought me back to reality.

As I gently moved the 2018 tassel to the left side of my cap and tossed it up into the air with the rest of my classmates, all the fear that made me want to run vanished. I no longer feel scared to be leaving high school and embark on a new adventure, but instead I felt proud.

I finally felt proud of myself.

Changing the Standard of Medicine, One Laugh at a Time

Samantha Cominelli

Western medicine was once known to be the best possible way of healing, but ideas on modern medicine are shifting, and alternative forms of medicine are becoming more popular. Despite its reputation for saving lives, Western medicine, or standard medicine, can be overwhelming; physicians often forget medical technology and machines are foreign to patients, scary, and uncomfortable (Cousins 152). Nonetheless, patients are kept in hospital beds, in close quarters with other patients, while they undergo ceaseless injections and blood tests. They are demoralized and stripped of their clothes and marked as "ill" with their hospital gowns. They are fed "cardboard" for breakfast, lunch, and dinner, and asked how they are feeling. They look up at the "Get Well Soon!" balloon given to them by their family, but all they can think of is "How am I supposed to get better in a place like this?" Nothing a hospital can bring is as helpful and comforting as homecare and natural healing methods (173), and Norman Cousins, the author of *Anatomy of an Illness as Perceived by the Patient*, is living proof of that.

At age 49, Norman Cousins was diagnosed with a sudden onset case of collagen disease, a crippling disease of the connective tissue in the body. He, like many with this disease, was admitted to the hospital and placed in the hands of the doctors. He had become a passive observer to his condition: accepting the doctor's initial treatment, despite his lack of improvement. When specialists told him that he had a one in five hundred chance of full recovery (33), he decided to take his treatment into his own hands. After collaborating with a physician who would finally listen to his needs, Cousins established a natural and noninvasive plan to treat his illness in which he would laugh in the face of death. Literally. Cousins believed ". . . there is a physiologic basis for the ancient theory that laughter is good medicine" (44), and he was not alone. Countless studies have agreed, claiming the benefits of alternative therapeutics. One physician, Lissa Rankin, explains how some of her patients, who have been failed by Western medicine, find hope in "alternative practitioners, including acupuncturists, homeopaths, and energy healers" (Rankin). Other studies on laughter therapy have shown improvement in mood state, self-esteem, and recovery of cancer patients (Kim et al. 217). With substantial evidence supporting alternative medicine, Cousins and his physician developed a plan where he would fight his disease with laughter, courage, and a few doses of vitamin C. Cousins uses *Anatomy of an Illness as Perceived by the Patient* as a platform to share his personal experience and beliefs in these forms of alternative medicine.

Anatomy of an Illness as Perceived by the Patient is one of the first books Cousins wrote addressing the revolutionary idea of a patient taking charge of their illness. Cousins broke down the wall between his doctor's verdict and his recovery, and by doing this, he teaches us how to do the same for ourselves. With its captivating philosophies, this book raises questions on our dependence on Western medicine as Cousins illustrates how powerful the body's natural recovery process can be. By sharing his personal experiences and the stories of others, readers feel as if they are walking alongside those on the road to recovery. Through this uplifting and inspirational piece, Cousins leads a movement for others to follow in his medical footsteps and changes the way we think of modern medicine and standard treatment.

Cominelli 3

Although some may be skeptical of his natural therapies, readers can be reassured by looking into Cousins's lifelong career of literature and science. Once earning a degree at Teachers College, Columbia University in New York City, Norman Cousins quickly took a job as a book critic for the *New York Evening Post,* and eventually became their managing editor. After years of writing for the *Post,* Cousins worked his way to editor-in-chief of the *Saturday Review of Literature.* With his strong literary background, Cousins became known for the integrity of his work and the philosophy to "not just appraise literature, but try to serve it, nurture it, safeguard it" (Colburn). After building his name, Cousins landed a job as a professor at the University of California, Los Angeles in the Department of Psychiatry and Biobehavioral Sciences. He taught courses in ethics and medical literature, as he continued to further his research of the human mind and body. He focused on the connection between an individual's attitude and health, as well as the biochemistry of human emotions (Pace). The beliefs he formulated during this time were put to use when his "progressive and incurable" (Cousins 33) disease began to take over his body. In the years after his recovery, Cousins continued to write, publishing two other works exploring the healing nature of the mind and body, known as *Head First* and *The Healing Heart*. Cousins's ideas are distributed all over the world, and his philosophies and therapies are practiced by many. Over his career, Norman Cousins was able to build up his integrity of words and credibility in medicine through his research and life experiences.

Cousins's *Anatomy of an Illness as Perceived by the Patient* is a perfect read for all. Despite the heavy scientific topic, Cousins writes in a familiar narrative, allowing an audience of all ages and interests to enjoy.

He writes his recovery and the recoveries of others who follow his practice through a casual voice, leaving no room for senseless medical jargon. With short chapters exploring areas of the mind, body, and spirit, Cousins continually raises questions in his readers' minds. This read is not only informative and engaging, but positive for all diagnosed with a chronic illness. Whether you are intrigued by the healing nature of laughter or a skeptic of its power, Norman Cousins's *Anatomy of an Illness as Perceived by the Patient* will make you think twice about the care you receive at the doctor's office.

Works Cited

Colburn, Don. "Norman Cousins, Still Laughing." *The Washington Post*, WP Company, 21 Oct. 1986, www.washingtonpost.com/archive/lifestyle/wellness/1986/10/21/norman-cousins-still-laughing/e17f23cb-3e8c-4f58-b907-2dcd00326e22/?utm_term=.121dca5a0d14.

Cousins, Norman. *Anatomy of an Illness as Perceived by the Patient*. W. W. Norton & Company, 2005.

Kim, So Hee, et al. "The Effects of Laughter Therapy on Mood State and Self-Esteem in Cancer Patients Undergoing Radiation Therapy: A Randomized Controlled Trial." *Journal of Alternative & Complementary Medicine*, vol. 21, no. 4, Apr. 2015, pp. 217–222. EBSCO*host*, doi:10.1089/acm.2014.0152.

Pace, Eric. "Norman Cousins, 75, Dies; Edited The Saturday Review." *The New York Times*, The New York Times, 1 Dec. 1990, www.nytimes.com/1990/12/01/obituaries/norman-cousins-75-dies-edited-the-saturday-review.html.

Rankin, Lissa. "Mind Over Medicine: How to Help Your Body Heal Itself." *Next Avenue*, Twin Cities PBS, 15 May 2015, www.nextavenue.org/mind-over-medicine-how-help-your-body-heal-itself/.

Ashley Rouleau
ENGL 114 T/R
Professor Lartigue
10 April 2018

Reform of the Electoral College

It is difficult to fathom just how radical an idea America's democracy was in the 18th century. Oligarchical elites controlled governments and people, and authority was derived from the "divine right of kings." Our Founding Fathers had to replace that authority with a new one, writing in the Declaration of Independence that governments would derive "their just powers from the consent of the governed." In modern day, this phrase has flourished to become profound and powerful. The clear implication is that our Founders believed that it was only through the process of achieving consent could a government be just; and that governments without consent would struggle to be not only just, but popular too (Rosenberg, 2016). As recent as the last Presidential election, there has been much talk of corruption and rigged political systems. I believe that it is in our country's best interest to investigate the flaws of the American voting system; and furthermore, work to refine those flaws. Specifically, the government should consider reform of the electoral college, which has anti-democratically granted more power to a body of electors than to the American people.

At the core of democracy lies a simple principle—that votes should count equally. The ideal is expressed as 'one person, one vote,' regardless. This principle, however, has been violated by the way that we coordinate Presidential elections. Because of the electoral college, votes are not weighed equally. It works as follows. States are assigned electors equal to the total number of representatives they have in Congress. This number is contingent upon how many U.S. senators and U.S. representatives each state has. While each state has two U.S. Senators, that does not hold true for the number of U.S. representatives, as this number can vary greatly depending on population size (U.S. Electoral College, n.d.). Because each state, regardless of population, gets the same number of senators, this inflates the power of small states relative to large states. For example, one vote in Vermont is worth 3.5 votes in Texas (Lessig, 2017). Residents of larger states, like Texas, are underrepresented. On the contrary, residents of smaller states, like Vermont, are overrepresented. In this way, the electoral college seems to be in conflict with the principles of democracy.

Unfortunately, there exists a much greater inequality by state law that has unjustly influenced the turnout of Presidential elections for as long as it has been in existence. It is referred to as the 'winner-take-all' rule of the electoral college. Every state, with the exception of Maine and Nebraska, 'assign all of their electoral college votes to the winner of the popular vote in that state—regardless of the margin by which that winner has prevailed' (Lessig, 2017). In the last presidential election, Donald Trump beat Hillary Clinton by just 10,000 votes (out of 4.6 million cast) in Michigan. Yet Trump received every single electoral college vote, while Clinton did not receive any (Lessig, 2017). States initially adopted 'winner-take-all' because it amplified the power of that state's vote, but when nearly all states had adopted this elector system, its effect became less to amplify and more to shift the focus of the presidential campaigns (Lessig, 2017). Under 'winner-take-all,' presidential candidates tend to put all their campaigning efforts towards the 'battleground states,' or the states in which the Democratic and Republican candidates have an equally likely chance of winning (Wikipedia, 2018). This explains the shocking statistic from the last presidential election—that nearly two-thirds of campaign events happened in just six states. Furthermore, fourteen states saw 99% of ad spending and 95% of candidate visits (Lessig, 2017). At the forefront of this issue, a majority of Americans are not promised a platform fitting to their desires. For example, Florida and Pennsylvania have a large senior citizen population relative to the nation as a whole (Lessig, 2017). Candidates, in striving to earn the votes of these seniors, will promise a platform that will strongly benefit that population. Likewise, battleground America is significantly more 'white' in comparison to the rest of America. Therefore, issues that are important to people of color tend to be neglected in battleground campaigns.

It seems pointless at best to continue to allow the electoral college to operate while still encouraging people to vote. As seen in the last Presidential election, the votes of 538 electors in the electoral college can, and ultimately will, override the popular vote of the people. Presidential candidate Hillary Clinton outpaced President-elect Donald Trump by almost 2.9 million votes; however, Donald Trump received more than the 270 electoral college votes needed to win (Krieg, 2016). This is not first time that the electoral college has overridden the people's will either. In the 2000 election, George W. Bush had fewer popular votes than Al Gore, yet Bush was the President-elect (Heuvel, 2008). Reform of the electoral college is necessary in order to preserve democracy. Foremost, we must modify the notorious 'all-or-none' principle of the 'winner-take-all' system. Instead of allocating all of a state's electoral college votes to the winner of the popular

Rouleau 4

vote, each state should be required to 'split' their electoral college votes, honoring each party fairly; and in turn, providing a more realistic distribution of the votes. For example, in Maine and Nebraska, two electoral college votes are assigned to the winner of the popular vote statewide and then one apiece to the winner in each congressional district (U.S. Electoral College, n.d.). This provides Democrats the opportunity to win one electoral vote out of conservative Nebraska, while Republicans have an opportunity to win one electoral vote from blue-leaning Maine. While this is only one alternate allocation strategy, the split-vote proposal takes away the power of 'winner-take-all.'

We must also equalize the power of one vote. To do so, we must take away the unsporting power that is given to smaller states in comparison to larger states. In regards to this particular problem within the electoral college, the only sound solution, in an effort to level the playing field for all voters across all states, would be to eliminate the electoral college completely. The setup of the electoral college does not allow a way for 'one person, one vote' to hold true, and it never will as long as population size remains relatively disproportional amongst the states. However, this proposition would be relatively hard to bring into effect. Because the electoral college is enshrined in our Constitution, getting rid of it would require a constitutional amendment. That is a two-thirds vote in both the House and the Senate and the ratification of three-fourths of the fifty states (Blake, 2016).

Although the electoral college is widely regarded as an anachronism, some people do believe in retaining the electoral college despite its lack of democratic pedigree. In regards to reform of the 'winner-take-all' system, a counterargument that advocates of the electoral college may present is that this system promises certainty of outcome. The electoral college creates a clear winner in cases where the popular vote is very close. Even the slightest plurality in a state will create a landslide electoral-vote victory, promising a definite winner in that state. However, the 'winner-take-all' system ultimately establishes an impractical margin between presidential candidates. In my opinion, the voice of the American people should take precedence over concern of whether or not the election will be a landslide victory. In reference to reform of the power of one vote in relation to state population size, those who defend the electoral college may argue that if we do away with the electoral college, the voice of smaller states would weaken. While this is certainly a feasible argument, the voice of smaller states would weaken only because they initially would of had, and still do have, more power in one vote.

The electoral college is a problem in American democracy. Unfortunately, it only appears to garner attention once every four years, and that is during election time. The Electoral College is an artificial device, but it has the fairy dust of history sprinkled on it. It conducts itself in such a way that the nation soon forgets that a majority of voters did not want George W. Bush as president and did not want Donald Trump either. As active citizens of the United States, we must fight for our voice in democracy. In doing so, we encourage fairer, more representative elections, and we are able to elect the presidential candidate of our choice, consensually.

Rouleau 6

References

Blake, A. (2016). Abolish the electoral college? Dream on, democrats. *The Washington Post.* Retrieved from https://www.washingtonpost.com/news/the-fix/wp/2016/11/09/getting-rid-of-the-electoral-college-dream-on-democrats/?utm_term=.397af4c06c5d

Heuvel, K. v., (2008). America needs electoral reform. *The Nation.* Retrieved from https://www.thenation.com/article/america-needs-electoral-reform/

Krieg, G. (2016). It's official: Clinton swamps Trump in popular vote. *CNN Politics.* Retrieved from https://www.cnn.com/2016/12/21/politics/donald-trump-hillary-clinton-popular-vote-final-count/index.html

Lawrence, L. (2017). The time has come: Reform the electoral college now. *The Daily Beast.* Retrieved from https://www.thedailybeast.com/a-second-paul-manafort-associate-has-turned-on-him?ref=scroll

Rosenberg, S. (2016). Three steps to modernize and reform American elections would help rebuild faith in our democracy. *U.S. News & World Report.* Retrieved from https://www.usnews.com/news/articles/2016-04-25/voting-reform-is-one-of-americas-biggest-challenges

U.S. Electoral College. (n.d.). What is the electoral college? Retrieved from https://www.archives.gov/federal-register/electoral-college/about.html

Wikipedia. (2018). Swing state. Retrieved from https://en.wikipedia.org/wiki/Swing_state

Natasha Jordan

Dr. Michaelian

College Writing 1

17 October 2017

It Is Not Just "Goodbye"

You are born in Norway. At five months old, your family moves to Turkey for two years, where your little brother is born. Your family then moves to Hong Kong and stays there for eleven years. Just when you start to feel like you can finally call someplace home, you get the news that you will be moving again. This time to Malaysia for five years. By the age of eighteen, you have lived in four different countries, but do not know which to call "home." On top of all this confusion, you have a blue passport, which makes you a citizen of the United States even though you have never lived there. You are finishing up your senior year of high school and now it is time to move again, this time away from your family, friends, high school, comfort, and away from everything you know.

Your life paints the perfect picture of a Third Culture Kid. Ruth Van Reken, co-author of *Third Culture Kids: Growing Up Among Worlds* and co-founder of *Families in Global Transition* conference, defines you as "a person who has spent a significant part of his or her developmental years outside the parents' culture(s). Although elements from each culture are assimilated into the TCK's life experience, the sense of belonging is in relationship to others of similar background" (Van Reken). A majority of your friends are also TCKs. They move around as much as you do, some even more, which means you are saying goodbye constantly, a process you are all too familiar with. It is never easy, and only gets harder the more you move. "TCK's don't lose one thing at a time; they lose everything at once" (Van Reken), your best friends, your environment, and the culture that you live in and experience. To say goodbye and transition from one location to another smoothly, you must reconcile, affirm those close to you, have a farewell moment, and think about your destination in a positive manner.

The first step in saying goodbye is reconciliation. This is the action of restoring relationships. If you got into an argument with your close friend or had a fallout with a classmate, it would seem easiest to just leave without fixing the problem, but you do not want to do this. Carrying regrets with you to your next destination is a lot more baggage than you have space for. Marilyn R. Gardner says it is "important to leave in peace, so we can begin in peace" (Gardner). It will not always be easy and can be uncomfortable in many situations. Working through conflicts, apologizing, and correcting your wrongs is a must do. As small as the problem may seem, it is important to resolve it so you can start fresh in your new location. Reconciliation is an action that you must pursuc in order to transition from one place to another smoothly. This step must occur before moving onto the following steps of saying goodbye.

The second step of saying goodbye and transitioning is affirming those who are close to you. Let that special person know he or she is important. Tell your best friends you are thankful for having them by your side through the breakups, hardships, and stupidity. Do not forget the fun memories you made like going to the gym after school and spontaneous smoothie runs. Let them know what they mean to you and that you are truly going to miss them. Write your coaches a letter, who have coached you for the past five years, about how they helped you grow as a person and athlete. Let everyone who impacted you know that they did. This step of affirmation may contain tears of joy, but also tears of pain as you acknowledge what others have done for you. Once you have told the important people in your life how much they mean to you, and the weeks until you depart have turned into days, it is time to move on to the third step of this process.

The third step in departing is the farewells. When you think of farewells, you think of that tight hug you do not want to let go of, because when you let go, you are letting go until the unknown. You are unsure of when you will see those who are close to you again. It could be tomorrow in the airport, or not for another twenty years; who knows when your paths will cross again, if ever. "The most painful goodbyes are the ones that we have never said" (Pelova). This might be the step you want to avoid because you believe it is easier to just move on, trust the author. The pain of not saying goodbye is a thousand times worse than the pain of saying it. Make time to go to your best friends' houses, give them that last hug, and say that final goodbye. Do not only depart with people but also with places, cultures, and traditions of the country you are leaving. If there is a path that you have run every morning for the past five years, run on it one last time. Walk through your school, where you spent many hours studying. Wander the streets of downtown, where you would grab late-night street food. Be in the moment and appreciate the comfortable environment around you, as very soon it will be gone, and you will be in a whole new country that you do not understand.

Now you have said goodbye to everyone and everything you know. As you are pulling out of your driveway, you hold back the tears in your eyes. The blurry shapes of your house fade into the distance as they become another memory. The most important thing for you to think about is where you are going which is the fourth and final step. To get through the process of transitioning from one country to the next you need to be thinking about your destination positively. New cultures, food, people, interactions, buildings, adventures, and much more. A world full of new things for you to explore. On your thirty-six-hour trip to the other side of the world, you are bound to have plenty of time to make a list of things you should do and places you should see. "Oh, the places you'll go! There is fun to be done! There are points to be scored. There are games to be won" (Seuss). As Dr. Seuss tells us, there are plenty of places for you to visit and new experiences to be had. Staying positive and thinking about your destination will make you feel better about your move. If you are moving to Italy, think of the delicious food that you will be able to eat, or to Thailand where the beaches will take your breath away. Positivity can distract your mind from everything you are leaving behind and negative emotions that come with moving.

This process of saying goodbye and transitioning from one place to the next is definitely a rollercoaster of emotions. Reconciliation, affirmation, farewells, and thinking positively about the destination are the four basic steps that you need to go through to smoothly, and most effectively get through the process. These steps were originally created for Third Culture Kids who move and "lose everything at once," but it is not limited to only them. For anyone who is moving, whether it is from New York to Massachusetts with your family or from Chicopee High School to Springfield College, these steps are applicable to you. This process is effective and can help you with your next move or transition, where you find yourself leaving many behind and are entering the world of the unknown. When saying goodbye is not enough or even too much, follow these steps for a smoother transition.

Jordan 6

Works Cited

Gardner, Marilyn. "Transition—Building a RAFT." *Marilyn R. Gardner*. WordPress, 22 May 2015. Web.

"Global TCK Care & Education." *Global TCK Care & Education-Creating Smooth Transitions—RAFT*. ICHED, n.d. Web.

Pelova, Anna. "The Importance of Saying Goodbye – Great Nomad." *Great Nomad*. Great Nomad, 27 June 2016. Web.

Pollock, David C., Ruth E. Van Reken, and Michael V. Pollock. *Third Culture Kids: Growing up among Worlds*. N.p.: Nicholas Brealey, 2017. Print.

Seuss. *Oh, the Places You'll Go!* N.p.: HarperCollins Children's, 2016. Print.

Van Reken, Ruth. *Cross Cultural Kids*. Ruth Van Reken, n.d. Web.

John Gatto
Professor Thifault
ENGL 113
18 December, 2017

Prisoners' Right to Education, Rehabilitation, and Work

It is estimated that there are over two million people who are currently imprisoned in United States correctional facilities. The U.S. not only has the highest incarceration rate of any other country, but also the quickest rising incarceration rate. Of this substantial number of inmates, a great amount of them have no job training or basic literacy skills prior to being incarcerated (Hall and Killacky 301). This brings up a very important issue: the U.S. needs to be educating these people and not just confining them. Prisons in the U.S. today are too focused on punishing the inmates and not enough on educating them and helping them rehabilitate and evolve as a human being. This ultimately results in high rates of recidivism, which is defined as the tendency of a felon to recommit a crime. It is also extremely difficult for people with felonies to obtain a job after being released from prison. This is significant because if two million people are in prison right now, then that means that even more people, including friends and families of these inmates, are negatively affected as a result of this. If the U.S. put more into the educating of inmates, then the substantial recidivism rate in this country would fall.

One issue with American prisons is that they do not necessarily straighten out inmates and change their lives for the better. Sheldon Seigafo says that, "America's prison population is commonly attributed to the U.S. Correctional system's failure to *correct* inmates," (183). Instead, these correctional facilities tend to concentrate on punishing inmates, which is likely to cause them to become threatening and unstable people. It is also worthy to note that cruel discipline has been happening since the beginning of humanity, and it has yet to be a very effective method of preventing crime. It may seem like giving criminals severe punishments would make them not participate in anymore illegal activities, when it truly is the exact opposite.

On the other side of the spectrum, one might say that these criminals deserve to be punished for the illegal actions they have committed. This may be a valid argument, however it does not have much evidence at all to help prove its claim.

Oftentimes people in general, not just felons, who face harsh penalties for their wrongdoings are not any less likely to keep performing those types of actions. For example, a fourth grade student gets in trouble at school for getting into a fight with another child at school. The parents of the child decide to ground him for three weeks. During this time period, the child may not watch television, play video games, eat dessert, or hang out with friends. This decision by the parents might have an effect on the kid's decision-making for the time being, but there is a low chance that it will prevent him from getting in any more fights. Instead, the parents should educate the child on why his actions were wrong, along with the effects his actions could have not only on him and his family, but the other child's family and even kids who were watching the fight as well. This is on a much smaller scale, but still comparable to someone who commits a crime and instead of receiving proper education and help, they get these extremely long sentences. While these sentences do "teach a lesson" to some extent, they should be used for not only educating, but rehabilitating prisoners. However, the U.S. Correctional system has yet to center their process around this rehabilitating (Seigafo 185), which brings up the point of inmates "right to rehabilitation."

People in correctional facilities deserve the right proper rehabilitation regardless of how awful a crime they committed. Every inmate who was interviewed in Hall and Killacky's study described their feelings of regret. "They also regret dropping out of school, engaging in criminal activity, and being confined in prison," (Hill and Killacky 306). While some prisoners choose to commit to illegal actions, nearly all of them never necessarily want to, but they have to in order to support themselves and/or their family. Here is an example of one inmate looked at in the study: "Nathan, who lost both of his parents by the time he was seven years old (his mother died and his father was incarcerated), was forced to sell drugs by his aunt who struggled to maintain her extended household. Despite Nathan's self-proclaimed passion for learning, he had to focus on selling drugs to help his aunt pay the bills," (Hill and Killacky 307). Many felons are dragged into a life of crime and warrant appropriate correction.

Some may argue that there is not much proof that more education for inmates helps them to not become habitual offenders. However, Hall and Killacky state that "the higher the educational attainment, the higher the reduction of recidivism," (302). To combat this perspective, studies have shown that only criminals who have obtained at least two years of a college education tend to get re-arrested at a rate that is 50% less than criminals that have no college education. Seigafo also says, "Inmates that have been rehabilitated during incarceration were reported to reintegrate and adopt crime free lives upon release," (186). If inmates were to receive legitimate opportunities for recovery, there would be a lot less of them returning to prison multiple times afterward.

Another considerable reason that ex-convicts reappear in prison is because of the level of difficulty in finding a steady job with a felony on record. "Inmates that have participated in the Returning Home project recounted that stable employment enabled them to be financially secure and prevented them from criminal activities, such as distribution of drugs for income," (Seigafo 190). Inability to find work after being released from prison can cause people to revert back to selling drugs just to put food onto the table for their families. People with a tarnished legal record should be eligible for the same jobs as people with clean records if they both have equal qualifications. If they have been properly rehabilitated in prison, then there is no reason why they should not be allowed to earn certain job positions.

Ultimately, the U.S. Correctional system needs to improve its higher education and rehabilitation programs. By doing this, the country would see lower rates of recidivism, which would cause less of a burden on the people who have been incarcerated along with their family and friends. Most of these people have no choice but to live a life of crime and regret all actions involved with that life. They deserve the right to education, rehabilitation, and work. All of this would make this country a better and safer place.

Works Cited

Hall, Renee Smiling, and Jim Killacky. "Correctional Education from the Perspective of the Prisoner Student." *Journal of Correctional Education,* vol. 59, no. 4, Dec. 2008, pp. 301–20. EBSCOhost, ezproxy.springfield.edu/login?url=https://search.ebscohost.com/login.aspx?direct=true&db=aph&AN=37588275&site=ehost-live.

Seigafo, S. "Inmate's Right to Rehabilitation during Incarceration: A Critical Analysis of the United States Correctional System." *International Journal of Criminal Justice Sciences,* vol. 12, no. 2, 2017, pp. 183–95, doi:10.5281/zenodo.1034656.

CPSIA information can be obtained
at www.ICGtesting.com
Printed in the USA
JSHW021308300720
6993JS00001B/1

9 781524 993818